# The Vanishing

D0732707

# The Vanishing

## Shakespeare, the Subject,

## and Early Modern Culture

Christopher Pye

Duke University Press   Durham & London

2000

© 2000 Duke University Press
All rights reserved   Printed in the United States of America on acid-free paper ∞
Designed by  C. H. Westmoreland   Typeset in Adobe Caslon by Tseng Information Systems, Inc.   Library of Congress Cataloging-in-Publication Data appear on
the last printed page of this book.

*To
Anna*

# Contents

# Figures

## List of Figures

# Acknowledgments

A modified version of chapter one appeared in *ELH* 61 (1994), 501–22; I am grateful to the publishers for permission to print the piece here. Chapter 2 was previously published in *Repossessions: Psychoanalysis and the Phantasms of Early Modern Culture,* ed. Timothy Murray and Alan K. Smith (Minneapolis: University of Minnesota Press, 1998); my thanks to the University of Minnesota Press for permission to republish. I want to thank the Cornell Society for the Humanities and Social Sciences for its fellowship support during the year in which I completed chapters 2 and 5. I also want to thank the Oakley Center for the Humanities at Williams College and all the participants in the Shared Research Seminar of which I was a part there. I delivered versions of chapters 2 and 4 as lectures for the Tudor and Stuart Society at Johns Hopkins University; I am very grateful for those opportunities and for the helpful responses I received on both occasions. I also thank the English Departments at Brandeis University and Dartmouth College for giving me an opportunity to present developing versions of the *Hamlet* chapter, and to the Center for Literary and Cultural Studies at Harvard University for the chance to present a version of chapter 3.

My personal debts are vast, and I'm happy for the chance to go some way toward acknowledging them here. I have been profoundly influenced in this project and inspired over the years by Anita Sokolsky, Steve Tifft, John Limon, and especially Karen Swann: my deepest debts are to them. Billy Flesch helped and encouraged every step of the way, in this and in everything. I am also deeply grateful to Tim Murray, Maud Ellman, Stephen Fix, Lyndy Pye, and Laurie Sokolsky for their long-term friendship and guidance. Though he's absolved of any relation to this project, my debt to Neil Hertz is in fact incalculable, which is to say too shamefully thoroughgoing to calculate. Scott McMillin opened the world of Renaissance drama to me and has influenced my readings ever since.

## Acknowledgments

I want especially to thank the manuscript's extremely helpful and inexplicably generous readers, and my editors—just as helpful, just as kind—at Duke University Press: Ken Wissoker and Richard Morrison. I also want to thank Ian Balfour, Ilona Bell, Kristy Carter-Sanborn, Joan Copjec, Jonathan Crewe, Grant Farred, Jonathan Goldberg, Judith Feher Gurewich, Stephen Greenblatt, John Guillory, Paul Held, Katie Kent, Regina Kunzel, Karen Newman, Laura Quinney, John Reichert, Frances Restuccia, Shirley Samuels, Mark Seltzer, Jim Shepard, Lisa Siriganian, and Shawn Rosenheim, as well as my students at Williams and Cornell, who have made so much difference.

# Introduction

This book is a series of forays into the problem of the subject in early modernity. I was drawn to questions concerning the status of early modern subjectivity not by any hope to settle them but by what seemed to me the intriguing starkness with which they had been answered by others. The argument for the historical character of subjectivity, for its being culturally defined: these are doxas of the current critical landscape. And yet, while a historicizing account of, say, late-nineteenth-century subjectivity might entail a fine-tuned analysis of shifting sexual ideologies, historicizing the early modern subject has in many instances meant asking whether there is a subject there at all, as if the fulsome Burckhardtian "complete man" of the Renaissance had yielded place to its spectral inverse: the pure nonsubject of early modernity. "At the center of Hamlet," Francis Barker asserts, "in the interior of his mystery, there is, in short, nothing."[1]

On the face of it, the one claim would seem as methodologically vexed as the other. While one can read in Jakob Burckhardt's full subject the projected image of nineteenth-century positivist historiography—a case of the historian getting his own back—one might equally ask from what transcendental posture outside his or her own cultural and subjective universe the contemporary cultural analyst claims descriptive access to a purely different being, a nonsubject or a presubject. More interesting, though, is the simple fact that such exemplary and radically divergent accounts—high humanist on the one hand, the most austere variant of cultural materialism on the other—should converge around the question of early modern subjectivity in particular. Is there something about the early modern subject that prompts such interpretive polarities? Indeed, is there something about early modernity as a category that complicates the entire project of "historicizing the subject"?

I'd like, in this preamble, to approach these larger questions about Renaissance subjectivity and history by reflecting on the methodological assumptions underlying the currently dominant cultural materialist and New Historicist approaches to the period, as well as on those underpinning social constructionism generally. The ascendancy of cultural materialism in early modern studies, and especially in accounts of the early modern subject, is evident enough from these recent titles: *Materialist Shakespeare,* edited by Ivo Kamps; Valerie Wayne's significant collection, *The Matter of Difference: Materialist Feminist Criticism of Shakespeare;* Linda Charnes's *Notorious Identity: Materializing the Subject in Shakespeare.*[2] Consider, too, materiality's anchoring, almost hypnotizing recurrences in some of the more condensed moments of theorizing in these works. Valerie Wayne cites Louis Althusser: "The existence of the ideas of [the subject's] belief is material in that his ideas are his material actions inserted into material practices governed by material rituals which are themselves defined by the material ideological apparatus from which derive the ideas of that subject."[3]

There is no mystery to matter's gravitational pull for a politically oriented account of the subject. "The materialist conception of the subject . . . aims," Jonathan Dollimore writes, "to challenge all those forms of literary criticism premised on the residual categories of essentialist humanism and idealist culture."[4] To "materialize" the subject is to counter those idealizing accounts that, implicitly at least, treat subjectivity as a transhistorical essence; to materialize the subject is thus to historicize it, to recognize its contingency and cultural embeddedness. According to such accounts, to acknowledge the fact of material determination is to discern the historical specificity of the Renaissance text. In an influential piece entitled "The Materiality of the Shakespearean Text," Margreta de Grazia and Peter Stallybrass suggest that the "fascination" exerted by an entire array of anachronistic post-Enlightenment fictions—the fiction of the author as origin, the fiction of the unitary work, the fiction of character as a supervening category—can in part be dispelled by an attentive return to the materiality of the Renaissance text: the material conditions of its publication; the varied, non-uniform nature of its material form; the old typefaces and spellings; the irregular line and scene divisions that obstinately remain to be "looked *at*" if not "seen *through.*"

What's implied by such a return to matter? The authors are at pains to insist that they are not offering a new myth of origination: "'The thing itself,'" they write, "the authentic Shakespeare, is itself a problematic category, based on a metaphysics of origin and presence that poststructuralism has taught us to suspect." What they nevertheless do claim to discover in the materiality of the text is something like the demonstrable evidence of the unfixed character of the Shakespearean text, the empirically determinable ground of its ungroundedness. The Renaissance text is to be found in all its historical particularity *there*, "outside metaphysics, in the materials of the physical book itself."[5]

It wouldn't be difficult to show how metaphysical the valorization of the physical book itself remains, how such textual empiricism amounts to the symmetrical inverse of the idealist categories—author, subject, and so on—the authors set out to undo. Indeed, while the antitranscendental intent of such analyses is clear enough, it is not entirely evident why the invocation of material contexts or practices should in itself be any less vulnerable to accusations of essentialism than idealizing accounts. If one is willing to recognize that the subject is a construct, shouldn't one be equally willing to acknowledge that "matter" is a construct, that materiality is derived?

In fact, by itself, the invocation of material causation needn't depart from the familiar cadences of high humanism, judging from the introduction to the recent collection *Subject and Object in Renaissance Culture*, edited by de Grazia, Stallybrass, and Maureen Quilligan. In an effort to recuperate critical attention for the object, the editors propose a hypothetical Hegelian derivation of the subject in its mutually creative relation to matter, a relation conceived outside any currently existing mode of production. Recognizing itself in the material it produces, the subject's being turns out to lie not in alienation or fetishism but "in suffering, in feeling its own corporeal and sensual receptivity as it intently plies its object," and, thus, in coming to recognize its object status in relation to other subjects.[6] Such a fantasy of mutual, sensual production elevates materiality at the expense of precisely what is radical in Marx's, or for that matter Hegel's, account: the fact that the subject-object relation is itself a contingency, the function of a prior and supervening structure, whether one reads that structure at the level of exchange relations or of the linguistic signifier.

Against those forms of materialist analysis that assume an unproblematically empirical and descriptive relation to a pre-modern subject (or nonsubject) one might set recent accounts that approach the early modern subject as an epistemological and dialectical category. In *Discovering the Subject in Renaissance England* Elizabeth Hanson argues powerfully that what emerges in the Renaissance is not so much a notion of interiority as such—as a number of critics have observed, such a notion can be traced back at least to Augustine—as "the usually fearful, even paranoid recognition that interiority can give the subject leverage against his world."[7] The alliance between inwardness and agency emerges during the Renaissance as the operations of discovery are brought to bear on another subject in a judicial context. "As one man examined another, searching for signs of hidden motives or loyalties, struggling to place him in the social order . . . he confronted as in a mirror the idea of the subject, not merely as authority's subordinate but as the origin of discourse and action, as a practitioner who is not fully expressed in the structures which constitute the givens of the world." What one sought in "the discovery scenario" was secret "intent" and, attending such a conception, "the possibility of a subject for whom certain claims, to authorial or to legal rights for instance, or to control over nature, might come to seem natural."[8] The subject in such an account is a worldly, contextual phenomenon to the extent that the scene of discovery is bound up with the era's judicial, legal, even scientific practices, but more generally insofar as it is conceived through its fundamentally contingent and strategic relation to the world.

In other words, according to Hanson's account, what emerges in early modernity is a hermeneutics of the subject, a subject understood within the (coercive) scene of its unmasking. And like all hermeneutic accounts, such a narrative is fraught with ambiguities. For Hanson, the problematics of the early modern subject arise at the point where discovery turns from an object to another subject, where the investigator encounters "as in a mirror" a subject as invested with agency as she is. But to cast the scene as an instance of intersubjective encounter

—a mirror scene—is in some sense to beg the question, for it implies that a subject was already there to be discovered. Thus Hanson also suggests that the subject is a function of the scene of discovery, that it is precisely in the structure of interrogation that a knowing subject is constituted. "The structure of interrogatory torture posits a victim in possession of hidden information that the torturer must struggle to uncover, and therefore produces a narrative of discovery, a movement from unknowing, through labor, to an encounter with truth."[9] To locate the subject there, as an effect, not a predicate, of the scene of its unmasking, is to suggest that subjectivity as such, whether that of the victim or the inquisitor, is a function of an investigative structure that precedes it. Or, more precisely, of the resistance that allows such a discovery-effect. In that sense, one would have to say that it is constitutively a barred subject, a subject by definition unknowable.

To conceive the subject as a function of its interrogation is ultimately to bring into high relief the reflexiveness attending the entire historical project of "discovering" the subject, or discovering the discovery of the subject: to what extent is such a project always a matter of positing in advance what one encounters there as if for the first time? When historicism takes the subject as its object, and especially when it turns its gaze to the era of the purported discovery of the subject, it encounters in heightened form the fact of its own rhetorical constructions.

Hanson acknowledges that fact even while resisting its implications:

An awareness of the rhetoricity of our own practices of cultural description is important so that we can choose our tropes wisely, conscious of the theoretical implications they carry. But, more crucially, it is necessary if we are to grasp the nature both of the phenomena which such work addresses, that is, cultural formations themselves, and of our own relation to them as objects of knowledge. The various slippages or repetitions that seem to beset the telling of the history of the subject testify to the impossibility of specifying when an epistemic formation is latent or burgeoning or fully achieved, or what its constituent elements are. If we go looking for the modern subject we will find signs of his "emergence" everywhere, but will be hard pressed to seize upon either the time and place of his birth or his definitive full-dress instantiation, because at any given moment in discourse the subject is situated within a unique, non-systematizable network of material pressures and intellectual filiations.[10]

Although Hanson speaks of the distinction between "trope and positivist assertion" and suggests that discursive accounts are necessarily a matter of "foreground[ing one] trope" as against another, the impossibility of determinately locating the subject turns out to be less a function of its inescapably tropical character—its "slippages," its "repetitions"—than it is of a mimetic inadequacy in the face of a "unique, non-systematizable" object—"material pressures," "intellectual filiations."

That mimetic recourse echoes the contradictions attending the range of work on early modern culture and subjectivity that is reliant on a more or less Foucauldian discursive model, including many New Historicist analyses. "Rather than erasing the problem of textuality, one must enlarge it in order to see that *both* social and literary texts are opaque, self-divided, and porous, that is, open to the mutual intertextual influences of one another," Jean Howard writes in her influential 1986 omnibus essay on Renaissance studies. "The ideological function of literature in a specific period can most usefully [be understood] by seeing a specific work relationally—that is, by seeing how its representations stand in regard to those of other specific works and discourses. . . . [To understand certain plays, for instance,] it may be important to see their representations of women in the light of the representations offered in masques, in conduct manuals, in medical treatises, and in Puritan polemics all written at approximately the same time."[11]

Howard's invocation of the textual, which is to say contingent and inscribed, character of historical phenomena is a valuable corrective to more literal-minded accounts of the material determination of early modern culture and subjectivity. And yet, however scrupulously textuality is noted in them, the persuasive force of such Foucauldian analyses tends to arise less from the discursive status of historical phe-

nomena than from the accumulation of discrete discursive instances
—the medical text, the juridical text, the conduct manual, and so
on—as if the empirical fact of multiplicity might at once counter
humanist universalism and acknowledge social difference, conveying
something of the endlessly rich texture of historical society as such.
"If we reject both the totalizing of a universal mythology and the
radical particularizing of relativism, what are we left with?" Stephen
Greenblatt asks in his account of the tale of Martin Guerre. "We are
left with a network of lived and narrated stories, practices, strategies,
representations, fantasies, negotiations, and exchanges that, along
with the surviving aural, tactile, and visual traces, fashion our experience of the past, of others, and of ourselves."[12]

But multiplicity is not difference, nor is it even opposed to "the
totalizing of a universal mythology." To read culture as an array of cumulable, and thus positively defined, even if mutually illuminating,
terms is to answer an essentialist account of the subject with a positivist account of the social domain. Understanding culture textually
or discursively, which is to say as in fact relationally defined, means
recognizing that every element is constituted *as* an element solely as
a function of the social/symbolic field within which it is inscribed,
or rather, in relation to the insistent failure of that field to constitute itself as a totality.[13] A fully or coherently anti-essentialist account
of culture implies not so much a claim for its multiple character, its
entailing "stories, practices, strategies, representations," as its hegemonic character, the fact that any cultural phenomenon exists always
in relation to a necessarily forced and unstable totalization of the social domain as such. In other words, an analysis of the subject as socially determined needs to be as scrupulous in its questioning of the
existence of society as a phenomenal category, as a given, as it is in its
questioning of the existence of subjectivity as a given.

Though I'm speaking generally, the argument for the importance
of understanding subjectivity in relation to the question of the social
domain—the social domain as a question—has particular force in relation to the problem of the early modern subject. For in a fundamental sense, it is with early modernity that "society" comes into being.
If we can speak of a modern subject, it is as a correlate of the radi-

cal social and symbolic transformation associated with the emergence of the modern state. "The *establishment of the political state*," Marx writes, "and the dissolution of civil society into independent *individuals*—whose relations with one another depend on *law*, just as the relations of men in medieval system of estates and guilds depended upon privilege . . . is accomplished by *one and the same act*."[14] The appearance of the abstractly defined, freely acting human subject—the contractual subject—is coterminus with the emergence during the early modern era of society understood as an autonomous, impersonal domain, the domain of state and law.

It is hard to overestimate the scope and nature of the transformation entailed in that institution of "society as such." "No description of the changes that have occurred in production, exchange and ownership could enable us to understand what is brought into play with the formation of the modern state," Claude Lefort writes. "It is the very *stage* of the social which *appears* at that point when political power is circumscribed *within* society, as the instrument which confers unity upon it, at that point where this power is supposed to originate from the very domain supposedly produced by its action. It is the institution of the social which is represented on this stage; and it is in the events that are acted out there, in the relations between individuals and groups, that the web of the 'real' may be found."[15] As an effect of the power that it produces, modern society is radically "deontologized," that is, inseparable from the question of its own staging. "The question of the genesis of the social," no longer a function of any transcendental reference, henceforth is "raised from the sphere of the social itself," a necessary and impossible project of figuring the social from within its own discursive place. The divisions entailed in that impossible, endlessly repeated autoconception open the very space of the social even while constituting modern society as a specifically *historical* society, a society founded in contingency, noncoincidence, and deferral, and thus one whose "reality" is synonymous with its historicity. "Social division and temporality are," Lefort remarks, "two aspects of the same institution."[16]

How might one imagine the subject in relation to such a transformation in "the web of the 'real'"? How conceptualize social subjectivity, not as a function of a pre-given or presumed social totality (in that sense, not even as socially constructed), but without reference to "society" as prior cause? I want to return to the early modern "discovery scenario" as Hanson describes it—the scene in which the subject is questioned but also posed as a question—focusing now on the cultural dream work of one of the more famously "interpellated" of Shakespeare's characters, one who has been a touchstone for critics who have understood subjectivity as an effect of cultural and material inscription:

> Be not afeard, the isle is full of noises,
> Sounds, and sweet airs, that give delight and hurt not.
> Sometimes a thousand twangling instruments
> Will hum about mine ears; and sometime voices,
> That if I then had wak'd after long sleep,
> Will make me sleep again, and then in dreaming,
> The clouds methought would open, and show riches
> Ready to drop upon me, that when I wak'd
> I cried to dream again.[17]

With its drifting voices and airs, this is, of course, a magic space, not a human one. And yet Caliban's evocation of the island world of *The Tempest* enacts in an exemplary form the very process of interpellation, of being solicited or brought into being as a desiring subject. It is all the more exemplary for its indeterminacy: Calling neither exactly from within nor from without, calling both to sleep and to waking, Caliban's "sometime voices" can be seen to figure the subject in its constitutive relation to the signifier, the locusless provocateur of the division, the fading and return that in a Lacanian account inaugurates the subject as split or unconscious.[18]

Read thus, does such an account etherealize or pastoralize the material and culturally specific causes of subjection? In fact, the material grounds of colonial subjection may be nowhere more evident than they are here, in the passage's promise of untold riches, as if it were in this dream within the manifestly dreamlike play that one momentarily "comes to" ideologically. In that sense, the scene might be read as the site of the contemporary audience's coming-to at least as much as it is the monster's. Manna for the cultural theorist as well, one might suppose: here's where the text harbors the promise of untold analytical capital, real matter for a properly materialist account of subjectivity.

But if all that is the case, it is worth noticing where those riches come from. By what process does an indeterminate humming about the ear settle in the course of the passage into the starker rhythm of dream and bereavement, of inwardness and loss? For with that movement there is also a shift from the floating signifier to the determined space of object-desire and to a subjectivity defined in relation to the promise of such a "commodified" object. The shift is marked by a slippage from conditional supposition ("That if I then had wak'd") to indicative assertion ("that when I wak'd"), as if the real stuff of desire, of loss, even of history, were enabled by an instance of self-forgetfulness—not forgetfulness of some prehistoric ground or condition but of the fictive or conjectural status of one's own speaking. Caliban's dream suggests that the encounter that brings the subject to—that interpellates—amounts to what Lacan terms "the encounter forever missed," the foreclosed supposition of an opening ("the clouds methought would open"), but more fundamentally the fading or detouring of the subject in the very movement of its coming forth.

Rather than being the function of a culturally specific interrogatory encounter, one might say the early modern subject is a subject insofar as it is the function of a missed encounter. The distinction is not a matter of material reality as against the inwardness of dreams, for Caliban's recounted dream is about the formative and always incommensurate juncture between subject and world, and about the derivation of a material ground. Indeed, the real cultural significance of such a constitutively missed encounter in relation to a culture claiming itself to be a culture of discovery, of endless first encounters, is evident enough, as it is for the mode of cultural analysis based on the frisson of such encounters.

But the more fundamental point concerns the very question of social or cultural causation. If we can judge from Caliban's narrative, the modern cultural subject—even the one imagined as other—is indeed bound up with and defined by the commodity, the always elusive object-cause of desire particular to a modern era. And yet, that unattainable object, precisely in its unattainability, both mimes and shores against a more radical contingency and noncoincidence. The aura of the commodity—its spellbinding magic not just in dreams—lies in this "quilting" or anchoring function in relation to the radically open field of signifiers, a function which constitutes subject and social domain alike.[19] In that sense, Caliban's dream is a modern dream, not because it exposes the material/cultural causes of subjectivity but because it *stages* such an origin and stages it explicitly as a foundational fiction.

Insofar as the modern conception of the individuated subject is coterminus with the emergence of society as such, essentialism and social constructionist might be seen as the symmetrical, even reinforcing, faces of the single, radical transformation that characterizes early modernity. Furthermore, because that transformation entails the binding of human subjectivity to its temporal historicity, to an always fictitious tale of its genesis, an account of the early modern subject can never amount to one instance among others of historicizing the subject. It would be more accurate to say that historicism and the early modern subject derive from the same ground. This is not to say that such a being is not historical, if we take historical to mean radically contingent. It is to suggest what the starkness of the oppositions characterizing the modern debate over the early modern subject—*the* subject/no subject, idealist/corporealist, essentialist/constructionist—symptomatically suggests: that the historicity of the early modern subject cannot be separated from the force entailed in giving it a genetic, narratable form.

It will be apparent by now the extent to which my account relies upon psychoanalytic theory, or theories. I have not framed the book by way of an outright defense of the application of that method to Renaissance texts, in part because that has been done so well by critics such as Elizabeth J. Bellamy,[20] in part because I believe the psychoanalytic preoccupation follows from a larger concern with the cultural and social dimensions of subjectivity: far from presuming a universal or ahistorical subjectivity, psychoanalytic language offers, I think, the most refined, least reductive means for articulating the contingency of the subject, its irreducible relation to sociality, to symbolic systems, to history.

But I also wanted to avoid casting this project as a matter of applying a distinct method—psychoanalysis—to a discrete object—the Renaissance. The relation between the two is revealing, I would argue, to the extent that it is more tangled. I agree with Stephen Greenblatt when, in his provocative, camp-forming argument against bringing psychoanalysis to bear on the Renaissance, he suggests that the subject of psychoanalysis—"our" subjectivity—is ultimately *a product of* the Renaissance.[21] I take that as a real insight and one that suggests what makes psychoanalytic theory so revealing in relation to early modernity. Precisely to the extent that psychoanalysis encounters its limits, or at least some version of a limit, in early modernity, it is capable of adumbrating the horizon of a distinctly modern episteme from within. The method that orients itself around such an encounter, or, more accurately, around such a scrupulously failed encounter, comes closer to the irreducible dimension of history, I would argue, than one that posits as if from on high a determined and unproblematic trajectory from one historical subjectivity to another. My approach will be distinct, then, from more universalizing applications of psychoanalysis to Renaissance texts insofar as it takes early modernity as a historical vanishing point of sorts. At the same time, it will be distinct from many historical accounts insofar as it avails itself of what theory, especially psychoanalytic theory, can say about the grounds of historicism itself.

The question of the validity of a psychoanalytic approach is bound up with questions a reader may already be asking: Why *the* early modern subject? Why not early modern subjectivit*ies*? I believe there are early modern subjectivities, just as, and at the same level as, there are ideologies—religious, national, and so on—and that the exploration of those subjectivities is vital. Nor do I believe at any level in a universal subject. The paradox is the same as the one that emerged in relation to the multiplying of cultural causes or discourses: To posit subjectivity as, in the final instance, multiple, as "subjectivities," is also to imply that subjectivity is a cumulative, determinate entity, a thing. And again, the determinable nature of the element presupposes the totalizable character of the social field in which it is constituted. At the same time, paradoxically, to speak of the subject—the subject precisely in its insistent failure to constitute itself as such—is to avoid a totalizing vision of its construction. Just as ideologies should be understood as they are constituted around and against a certain impossibility immanent in the social, so subjectivities should be understood not just empirically but in the precise and distinct ways in which they articulate themselves around that point of subjective impossibility. It is in that articulation that the social and cultural subject appears.

The chapters that follow approach the problem of the subject by pursuing intersecting paths through a range of materials and representational forms: pictorial as well as literary works; religious as well as secular material; high and low cultural phenomena, including witchcraft, anatomical treatises, the marvelous bric-a-brac of the "wonder cabinet." My choices are not intended to have a summary or even necessarily a representative relation to early modern culture. Instead, in each instance I'm interested in teasing out those limit-points of symbolization where, I will argue, the cultural and sexual contours of the early modern subject come into view. My recurring literary focus will be Shakespeare. I would defend the emphasis heuristically: For any number of good and bad reasons Shakespeare amounts to a familiar "common ground." But that's probably just a way of saying it's the ground with which I'm most familiar. While I do feel that Shakespeare's texts offer a remarkably developed account of the subject and of the mechanisms of social and symbolic interpellation, I am certainly not claiming that they have a defining relation to modern subjectivity. At the same time, I would argue against the implicit sociologism of the assumption that one can come to terms with something like the problem of the subject through an empirically "representative" sampling. To argue (rightly) against claims for the universality of Shakespeare's work does not preclude the possibility that his work is at least as telling about, say, subject formation as anyone else's.

In the first chapter I consider arguments for the distinctly economic character of early modern subjectivity, arguments central to some of the most forceful claims for the socially constructed nature of the modern subject. Looking to the earliest moments in Shakespeare's Histories, and the earliest moments of his own writings as well, I will argue that in fact the early modern subject emerges not as a commodified being in a system of exchange but at the more radical and unstable point where economy establishes itself *as* a system. By tracing subject formation to such a point, I demonstrate how the economic character of the early modern subject is bound up with the very question of its historicity. The scene of subjective emergence, luridly associated with the irruption of the demonic into chronology, suggests that the early modern "economic" subject be understood not simply as a historical datum but as coterminus with and implicated in our own distinctly modern modes of historical understanding.

Picking up on the significant "demonic" element in the scene of subject formation, I turn in the second chapter to the witchcraft phenomenon itself and suggest that it should be understood not simply as an empirical phenomenon but in relation to the problematic character of the social domain as such. Tracing witchcraft in its relation to the body politic, as well as its relation to the body of the subject possessed, I will argue that demonism is intimately bound up with a significant shift in law and symbolic order, a shift that coincides with the emergence of an abstract social field during the early modern era. At the level of the subject, that transformation is particularly evident in the domain of vision and sexuality; along these lines, I associate the concept of demonic "fascination" with the erotic dimensions of the emergent social subject. Following a path from the odd part-objects involved in the rites of witchcraft to the conjured appearance of a charged bodily remainder at the center of Michelangelo's *Last Judgment*—one of the era's most vaunted evocations of the universal order of things—I suggest the untoward sexual and gendered underpinnings of the modern speculative subject.

In chapters 3 and 4 I consider directly the mechanism of subjective interpellation, the process by which a subject is symbolically and historically inscribed. Chapter 3 begins with characteristically Renaissance pictorial representations of what I take to be the ur-instance of symbolic interpellation in Western tradition: the Annunciation, the scene in which Mary is hailed and called into her sacred narrative destiny. Although having arisen in a world very different from Reformation England, these works are pertinent in part because they articulate for the first time, paradoxically, an iconoclastic logic at the heart of modern, secular identity. Continuing to focus on matters of sexuality and vision, I examine what is significant about the fact that these overtly gendered annunciatory scenes represent the emergence of the vanishing point in especially pure form: a pictorial structure that articulates the modern subject as defined in relation to its own negation. I then consider the famously galvanizing Dover Cliff scene from *King Lear*, in which once again subjectivity is visibly constituted, or reconstituted, around the determinate infinity of the vanishing point, although now in a scene explicitly affiliated with demonic possession and revealing of the emerging relationship between fantasy and the political state as structuring categories. It is within the context of such a structural transformation that one can recognize the complicity between the vanishing point as an interpellating or subjectivizing mechanism, the organizing role of the "barred woman," and the emergence of a distinctly modern concept of history as built around a spatial/temporal horizon.

There is no end, of course, to what *Hamlet* has meant and no attitude to assume toward it except the shamefully supererogatory. By proposing that the play is in a fundamental sense *about* interpellation, I suggest in chapter 4 that the work's historical aspect cannot be dissociated from the history and form of its peculiar interpretive solicitousness. Beginning with one of the most famous of the modern interpretive crises occasioned by the play, I suggest that the play articulates an early modern subjectivity again consistent not only with the emergence of the abstract state but also, inseparably, with an emerging homosocial economy associated with the modern "man of letters." The play stages that "new," presumptively male, subject, one affiliated with abstract law, against a more "archaic" order associated with structures of political and psychic incorporation. That advent is, I argue, not less real for its being retroactively posited.

In chapter 5 I return to the concerns of the first two chapters—commodification, exchange, fantasy, and subject formation—but now by turning from the subject to the object, or rather, to early modern "matter." Moving between the Renaissance "wonder cabinet," the famous "closet scene" in *Hamlet* (one of the primal scenes of psychoanalysis), and Marx's account of the advent of the exchange relation, I suggest that the emergence of matter, the recalcitrant stuff that limns the pre-empirical subject, is bound up with a radical transformation in the body politic: the process of political disincorporation. Complicating the premises of cultural materialist analysis, I argue that such matter is not the empirical ground but the phantasmatic condition and the limit of historicist inquiry.

# Chapter 1

## The Theater, the Market, and

## the Subject of History

Nothing has so marked recent efforts to establish the historical contours of early modern subjectivity as the perceived relationship between economy and representation. In *Worlds Apart*, Jean-Christophe Agnew suggests how implicated the worlds of the theater and the market were during the period and how central both were to early modern accounts of identity. With the advent of exchange-value as a property independent of use-value, the marketplace evolved from a localized institution into a supervening process capable of reconstituting the very society that set it in motion. "To those caught up in this expanded circulation of commodities of the early modern epoch," Agnew writes, "the very liquidity of the money form—its apparent capacity to commute specific obligations, utilities, and meanings into general, fungible equivalents—bespoke the same boundless autonomy that Aristotle had once condemned as an unnatural, 'chrematistic' form of exchange."[1] According to Agnew's account, in sixteenth- and seventeenth-century England the newly liquid market conspired with the protean character of theater to prompt a "crisis of representation" bearing on identity as such. "The new drama showed, as no other genre could, how precarious social identity was. . . . By deliberately effacing the line between the self's iconic representation in art and ritual and its instrumental presentation in ordinary life, Renaissance theater formally reproduced the same symbolic confusion that a boundless market had already introduced into the visual codes and exchange relations of a waning feudal order."[2]

Literary critics concerned with the economic determinations of cultural productions have figured this crisis in terms of an increasingly unbounded process of social commodification. Thus Don Wayne's reassessment of "Drama and Society in the Age of Jonson" turns on the dramatist's inability to imagine himself fully independent of an "emerging commodity system of economic and social exchange," and Karen Newman reconceives the woman's role within drama of the era in terms of a generalized structure of consumption: "She is represented in the discourses of Jacobean London as at once consumer and consumed."[3] The centrality of the economic perspective in these accounts has considerable—even shrill—empirical support. Consider the not-so-obscurely intertwined proliferation of antitheatrical and anti-usury tracts during the era, each declaring the limitless shame of a cultural transformation that threatened to reduce all to a groundless play of terms.

Yet it is precisely the sweeping nature of such a transformation that raises methodological qualms. It is the constitutive force of economy—the prospect that one might be reduced to a commodity or mere factor in a system of exchange—that prompts fear and shame. But isn't apprehension precisely what guarantees one's externality to the threatened transformation? From what position can one perceive one's own commodification with anxiety? The problem of registering the empirical ground of a constitutive transformation can similarly be posed at the level of structure: how is it possible to speak of the origins of a transformation that reconstitutes the society that institutes it, thus, in a sense, effacing its own causes?

Paradoxically, economy's tendency toward a certain ungroundedness has if anything silently underwritten historicism's most recent avatar, New Historicism. The writings arrayed under that heading are bound together in part by their reliance on the ease with which economic description seems to lend itself to a generalized metaphorics of speculation and exchange, to a certain discursive liquidity.[4] Here is Stephen Greenblatt's account of the relationship between a historical document—the report of the wreck of a merchant ship written by a company man—and a literary work—*The Tempest:* "The changes I have sketched are signs of the process whereby the Bermuda narrative is made negotiable, turned into a currency that may be transferred from one institutional context to another. The changes do not constitute a coherent critique of the colonial discourse, but they function as an unmooring of its elements so as to confer upon them the currency's liquidity."[5] Freed from the particularities of the market, the discourse of negotiation, liquidity, and exchange comes to sustain an account of the entire social field, all under the inclusive rubric of "the circulation of social energies."

In this case, one is prompted to ask not so much what grounds economy as what gives it its apparently limitless alchemical powers as a descriptive term. The effectiveness of New Historicism's cultural—or economic—poetics, its capacity to seem at once historically particular and boundlessly expansive, depends both on the residual empirical aura that clings to such economic language and, as importantly, on economy's distinctive ability to dissimulate its status as a system. In reading Greenblatt's account, one is struck by the combination of fungibility at the level of discrete phenomena and of totalizing force at the level of the social field itself, a globalization most evident when the cultural exegete is most at pains to banish it: "The circulation of social energy by and through the stage was not part of a single, coherent, totalizing system. Rather it was partial, fragmented, conflicted. . . . What then is the social energy that is being circulated? Power, religious awe, free-floating intensities of experience: in a sense, the question is absurd, for everything produced by the society can circulate. . . . Under such circumstances, there can be no single method, no over-all picture, no exhaustive and definitive cultural poetics."[6] No single method or overall picture, that is, except the most embracing: the economic concept of circulation itself. Whether at the level of the discrete subject or at the level of the social field, whether applied literally as final cause or figuratively as global function, the economic metaphor seems to allow for a comprehensive account of the loss of totality, the fantasy of cultural science itself, perhaps.

To explore the relations among economy, theater, and subjectivity in the Renaissance, I turn to a moment early in Shakespeare's theatrical career: act 1, scene 4 of the dramatist's earliest and most dazzlingly unformed play, *Henry VI, Part 1*. The scene suggests that both in and beyond the stage a subject is indeed constituted in economic terms. It also shows how intimately theater is involved in the process of subject formation. But theater and market assume their constitutive power—the subject emerges—only at the point where economy altogether exceeds itself as empirical ground and as totalizing function. Not simply inscribed within an already fully constituted economic domain, not simply commodified, the early modern subject is coterminous with the unstable "founding" of the economic function itself. The politics of subject formation, its relation to nationalism, to sexuality, and to a distinctly modern conception of history, should be understood, scene 4 suggests, in relation to that radical, systemic horizon.

I

Act 1, scene 4 of *Henry VI, Part 1* is notable for the appearance of the French heroine, Joan of Arc—or "Pucelle," as she is called—and for the way the emergence of that figure serves to galvanize the otherwise peculiarly drifting beginnings of the play and of the Histories. Shakespeare's Histories begin with an ending, with their own ending, in a sense. The curtain opens on the funeral of Henry V, the absolute sovereign whose glorious conquests the last play of the cycle celebrates. Even before the body is buried, word arrives from France of the dissolution of the Empire, culminating with an account of the betrayal and capture of England's warrior hero, Lord Talbot. The play then shuttles back and forth between the French troops, who are temporarily emboldened by the appearance of the warrior-maid, and scenes of political disarray in England.

At the start of act 1, scene 4 England's fortunes seem to have reversed themselves again, at least momentarily. Talbot has been ransomed from captivity and, as the scene opens, stands with his companions on a turret overlooking Orleans, the siege of which they are planning confidently. But a canon on the lower stage ignites, felling Salisbury and Gargrave, two of Talbot's comrades on the tower. Almost simultaneously, a messenger arrives to announce the approach of the "holy prophetess," Pucelle. Mere word of her arrival suffices to raise the dead: "Here Salisbury lifteth himself up and groans."[7] Nevertheless, and despite temporary setbacks, Talbot and the play

itself assume a minimally coherent trajectory, for the first time, in relation to this threat:

> Hear, hear how dying Salisbury doth groan;
> It irks his heart he cannot be reveng'd.
> Frenchmen, I'll be a Salisbury to you. (1.4.103–5)

Talbot's heroic exploits against Pucelle and the French go on to
become the formal core of an otherwise stunningly fragmentary
chronicle.

The structure of the scene is a familiar one: a threat from without is used to coalesce forces within, in this instance invoking a sense
of national and literary identity. The scene is equally noteworthy for
the way in which it draws together the theater and the market. The
scene that concludes with Pucelle's charged appearance begins with
one of Shakespeare's most explicit articulations of the intimate relationship between market and spectacle. Appearing for the first time
in the play, Lord Talbot discourses on his recent treatment in captivity
by the French:

> With scoffs and scorns and contumelious taunts
> In open market-place produc'd they me
> To be a public spectacle to all. (1.4.39–41)

The uneasy correspondence between the shaming effects of display
and commodification that energized the antitheatrical polemics of
the age comes into plain view here, presumably because it has been
displaced onto the French.

Indeed, Talbot's escape from the French amounts to a victory over
the depredations of exchange and theatricalization alike. "By what
means got thou to be releas'd?" Salisbury asks. Talbot answers:

> The Earl of Bedford had a prisoner
> Call'd the brave Lord Ponton de Santrailles,
> For him was I exchang'd and ransomed.
> But with a baser man of arms by far
> Once in contempt they would have barter'd me;
> Which I, disdaining, scorn'd, and craved death

Rather than I would have been so pill'd esteem'd;
In fine, redeem'd I was as I desir'd. (1.4.27–34)

Talbot holds out for an exchange worthy of his class and honor. But
he does more. Wagering the absolute term of his own death to ac-
complish the substitution he desires, Talbot controls and thus situates
himself outside the blind denominations of exchange and so gives exchange a faintly theological surplus, as the language of redemption
suggests. Theater here is staked on class difference, for by maintaining
at the risk of his life the all-important distinction between aristocratic
ransom and the leveling and depletionary exchanges of a newer order,
Talbot preserves a redeeming, if minimal, difference between the English stage—the display the audience sees before it—and the site of
the market.

Talbot's narrative of the spectacle in the market gives local form
to a more submerged and troublingly expansive version of surrogacy
associated with the English hero in the scene and the play, an unbounded representational economy that the scene will engage in detail
before returning once again, with Talbot's first victory, to a concrete
and familiar thematization of the market. "Talbot, my life, my joy,
again return'd?" Salisbury exclaims from the upper stage as the hero
enters for the first time (1.4.23). This is the language of redemption,
perhaps. But the timing of the proclamation—from the moment he
first appears, Talbot is "again return[ing]"—and the heightened re-
flexivity of the moment—"Discourse, I prithee, on this turret top"
(26)—produces the impression that the hero's appearance coincides
with the more insistent and quotidian reiterations of theater itself, in
which the most momentous arrival amounts to a return. The impression is heightened by Talbot's oddly recurrent destiny in the play. The
audience first hears of him when a messenger interrupts the opening
funeral to announce that at the siege of Orleans Lord Talbot has been
encircled by the enemy, betrayed by one Sir John Falstaff, and, one is
momentarily given to believe, slain. In fact, he is taken prisoner. And
yet, Talbot's fate *does* conclude when he is once again encircled by the
enemy, once again betrayed by Sir John Falstaff, and, this time, slain.

We can make sense of Talbot's reiterative and reflexively theatrical status in the play by recognizing how bound up his fate is with the problem of origins in this originative drama—the first of the Histories, the first of Shakespeare's career. In beginning with the funeral of Henry V, the entire history cycle shores and initiates itself, in principle, against the absolute measure of the sovereign's death. Nothing, however, could be less stable than the king's demise. The lords respond to news of the empire's fragmentation:

| | |
|---|---|
| Bedford: | What say'st thou, man, before dead Henry corse? |
| | Speak softly, or the loss of those great towns |
| | Will make him burst his lead and rise from death. |
| Gloucester: | Is Paris lost? Is Roan yielded up |
| | If Henry was recalled to life again, |
| | This news would cause him once more yield the |
| | ghost. |

(1.1.62–67)

Rising to die again, reviving and ceasing in the same instant, Henry's return would only riddle death's limit and guarantee. The entire trajectory of the Histories, in which the sovereign does indeed return but through a double, lineal, and cyclic form, can be seen to answer to this radical equivocation at the source.[8] Talbot's "again return[ing]" and his surrogacy should be understood in relation to the King's ghostly wavering. To initiate themselves at all, the Histories must check the prospect of limitless reiteration and of a boundless form of exchange that marks and derides their advent. Rather than simply enacting a narrative of nationalist exploits, Talbot is burdened with the task of generating in its sparest form the very possibility of a vectored and narratable history out of representation's empty returns.

From the moment he appears, "Talbot" is to a remarkable extent a theatrical construct. "Again return'd," he tells his tale, a tale of specular aggression and counter-aggression:

> With scoffs and scorns and contumelious taunts
> In open market-place produc'd they me
> To be a spectacle to all:
> Here, said they, is the terror of the French,

The scarecrow that affrights our children so.
Then broke I from the officers that led me,
And with my nails digg'd stones out of the ground
To hurl at the beholders of my shame.
My grisly countenance made others fly
None durst come near me for fear of sudden death. (1.4.39–48)

It is specifically as a terrible spectacle, and in retaliation against those who would reduce him to such a spectacle, that Talbot displays the martial ferocity that historically defines him.

As Talbot continues his discourse, the theatrical aggressivity he recounts is gradually and complexly concatenated with his immediate position on stage before us. The scene is framed by an exchange between the French Master Gunner and his son in the besieged city down below. The Dauphin's "espials" have informed the Master Gunner

How the English, in the suburbs close intrench'd,
Wont through a secret grate of iron bars
In yonder tower to overpeer the city. (1.4.9–11)

To "intercept this inconvenience," the Master Gunner has placed "a piece of ord'nance" below on the stage proper aimed toward the grate in the tower where Talbot now stands (1.4.14–15). The boy reappears below as Talbot completes the discourse on his captivity:

In iron walls they deem'd me not secure;
So great fear of my name 'mongst them were spread
That they suppos'd I could rend bars of steel,
And spurn in pieces posts of adamant;
Whereof a guard of chosen shot I had
That walk'd about me every minute while;
And if I did but stir out of my bed,
Ready they were to shoot me in the heart.
*Enter the Boy with a Linstock* (1.4.49–57)

At this point, the boy appears, as if the materialization of Talbot's victimizers. But in the interval between the boy's entrance, his lighting of the ordinance, and its detonation, the relations of power figured in Talbot's account are reversed. Vowing revenge on the English hero's captors, the men turn their gaze on the city spread before them, that is, out over the stage toward the audience.

Salisbury:  I grieve to hear what torments you endur'd,
              But we will be reveng'd sufficiently.

            ·  ·  ·  ·  ·  ·  ·  ·  ·  ·  ·

              Here, through this grate, I count each one,
              And view the Frenchmen how they fortify.
              Let us look in, the sight will much delight thee.

            ·  ·  ·  ·  ·  ·  ·  ·  ·  ·  ·

Talbot:     For aught I see, this city must be famish'd
              Or with light skirmishes enfeebled.
              *Here they shoot, and Salisbury falls down*
              *[together with Gargrave]*
Salisbury:  O Lord, have mercy on us, wretched sinners!
Gargrave:  O Lord, have mercy on me, woeful man!
Talbot:     What chance is this that suddenly hath cross'd us?
              Speak, Salisbury; at least if thou canst, speak.
              How far'st thou, mirror of all martial men?
              One of thy eyes and thy cheek's side struck off!
              Accursed tower! accursed fatal hand
              That hath contriv'd this woeful tragedy! (1.4.57–77)

Whose contriving hand, exactly? Talbot's, perhaps. For the shot that rends the "secret grate of iron bars" erupts precisely at the moment when the figure who threatened to "rend bars of steel" in revenge against those who reduced him to spectacle turns outward and reduces all beneath his masterful gaze. But the metatheatrical element of the scene—"accursed fatal hand / That hath contriv'd this woeful tragedy"—signals a more radical uncertainty about the grounds of this stagy violence. For the moment Talbot "overpeers the city," overlooking the canon below and gazing out beyond the stage, is also the moment the audience finds its own masterful and subjecting gaze returning on itself. The elaborate calculus of theatrical relations that constitutes Talbot's history works toward, or perhaps devolves from, this single instance of transgression, the moment spectacle returns the gaze, and the boundary between viewer and spectacle is rent.

Hardly an accident or a device, that reversal of object and gaze follows from and is inherent in the very economy of the theatrical. To the extent that the viewing subject defines itself in reducing all to spectacle—insofar as the subject is itself a function of the initiatory division between seer and seen—spectacular power will invariably amount to a reversionary transgression, a violent and renewed revenging home. The oddly exact wound resulting from this stagy disruption—"one of thy eyes and thy cheek's side struck off"—can be read as the disquieting image of the audience's divided and specular formation.

By all rights, the movement of mirroring exchanges should close itself off with that disastrous redounding, but for a detail: The violence does not return exactly home. The shot intended to intercept the overmastering onlookers is, in turn, intercepted, for it is not Talbot, who discoursed about rending barriers and revenging beholders, but his auditor, Salisbury, who suffers the violent returns. The effects of that misfire can be felt in the subterranean workings of Talbot's impromptu eulogy:

> In thirteen battles Salisbury o'ercame;
> Henry the Fift he first train'd to the wars;
> . . . . . . . . . . . . .
> Yet liv'st thou, Salisbury? Though thy speech doth fail,
> One eye thou hast to look to heaven for grace;
> The sun with one eye vieweth all the world.
> . . . . . . . . . . . . .
> Bear hence his body, I will help to bury it.
> Sir Thomas Gargrave, hast thou any life?
> Speak unto Talbot, nay, look up to him.
> Salisbury, cheer thy spirit with this comfort,
> Thou shalt not die whiles—
> He beckons with his hand and smiles on me
> As who should say, "When I am dead and gone,

Remember to avenge me on the French."
Plantagenet, I will. . . .

. . . . . . . . . . . . .

Wretched shall France be only in my name. (1.4.78–97)

Through the dying Salisbury, Talbot receives—or ventriloquizes—the injunction that constitutes his martial identity—"avenge me on the French"—and, through the irreversibility of that loss, is able to stabilize the movement of exchange for the first time: "Frenchmen, I'll be a Salisbury to you" (1.4.106). But that call to martial and national destiny is posed against signs of disquiet. Before the final beckoning, Talbot invokes his companion, buries him, then reinvokes him again. He enjoins Salisbury to exchange gazes with the mirroring sun, with the dead or dying Gargrave, with every specular gaze except that of the true "mirror of all martial men," himself.

Such wavering may be psychologized as Talbot's guilty response to the death of the man who stood in his place and intercepted his fate. But what Talbot turns from exceeds the economy of guilt and shame altogether: "He beckons with his hand and smiles on me / As who should say, 'When I am dead and gone, / Remember to avenge me on the French.'" The martial hero's history is grounded at its source on a critical misreading. Both more benign and more alarming than an agonistic call to revenge, Salisbury's smiling and beckoning represents the logical completion of the circuit of exchange in the workings of the death drive. To close off the movement of substitutions and assume his proper place—to come into his own—requires the simple and impossible expedient of taking up the position of the dead man who had stood in his place. Not, or not merely, a reflection of guilt, the spectral solicitation confirms the more fundamental truth of Talbot's inscription within a representational economy that exceeds and defines him. Earlier, Talbot had "craved death" rather than submit to exchange. Here, he is shown to crave death precisely to the extent that he *is* a function of exchange, of an economic circuit that travels beyond any conceivable limit.[9]

It is in relation to this solicitation of the death drive—the phantasmatic sign of a splitting within—that we should understand the abrupt appearance of a demonic force from without. No sooner has Talbot received, and refused, the fatal sign than news arrives of Pucelle's approach. Salisbury's flickering returns are now transformed into a more lurid automatism:

> Wretched shall France be only in my name.
> *Here an alarum, and it thunders and lightens*
> What stir is this? What tumult's in the heavens?
> Whence cometh this alarum, and the noise?
> *Enter a messenger*

| | |
|---|---|
| Messenger: | My lord, my lord, the French have gather'd head. |
| | The Dolphin, with one Joan de Pucelle join'd, |
| | A holy prophetess new risen up, |
| | Is come with a great power to raise the siege. |
| | *Here Salisbury lifteth himself up and groans* |
| Talbot: | Hear, hear, how dying Salisbury doth groan! |
| | It irks his heart he cannot be reveng'd. |
| | Frenchmen, I'll be a Salisbury to you. (1.4.97–106) |

Displaced outward to the French and to the demonized woman, the power to revive the dead reappears in an overcharged and exclamatory form—as conjury. The splitting within, manifest as an alarming call to quiescence, is now recast as a more familiar and more manageable national and sexual antagonism. Pucelle takes on all the coded and recognizable ambiguities of the castrating woman. "I know not where I am, nor what I do," Talbot exclaims, "A witch by fear, not force . . . conquers as she lists" (1.5.20–22).

With this displacement outward, the field of power also shifts from the specular to the linguistic or symbolic register. The demonic woman is explicitly a phallic woman, and, for all her actual prowess in combat, the stakes of the martial confrontation that ensues center on the more fundamental issue of symbolic mastery. Pucelle's potency is first visible less in her literal power to raise the dead than in the linguistic mechanism that calls up that event as if of its own accord: "A holy prophetess new *risen up,* / Is come with a great power to *raise* the siege. / *Here Salisbury* lifteth himself up *and groans.*" Although affiliated with the woman and the unanchored potencies of the demonic, such effects transpire entirely within the terms of the paternal order. While Talbot announces "wretched shall France be only in my name," it is the phallic maid whose words initially assume that performative power associated with the name of the father: "Rescu'd is Orleance from the English! / Thus Joan de Pucelle hath perform'd her word," Pucelle herself declaims (1.6.2–3). Talbot's victory is sealed not when he overcomes but when his name does.

> Soldier: The cry of Talbot serves me for a sword,
> For I have loaden me with many spoils,
> Using no other weapon but his name. (2.1.79–81)

The victory takes no time—a few scenes and a few skirmishes. For, despite the hyperbolic powers of the witch, the threat is already allayed from the moment it entered the field of gendered sexuality. Neither, one might conjecture, does the direst risk coincide with the specular dimensions of the scene, whatever the genealogical progression from spare and violently unstable theatricality to safely thematized martial victory might suggest. Specular subversion, like symbolic castration, implies its own mechanism for articulating a subject, however volatile and contradictory. Instead, the danger around which the scene is structured occurs at the point where genealogy yields to return and where all the articulatory resources of theater—specular and linguistic, imaginary and symbolic—encounter their limit in the mute workings of the death drive. With Talbot's refusal of that solicitation, and with the displacements that follow from that disavowal, representation is checked at its limit, and a national, as well as personal and sexual, identity coalesce for the first time.[10]

The significance of Talbot's apostrophe on the turret top may be measured in the extent to which the entire, strangely reiterative movement of his career gravitates back to and rewrites the scene. In Talbot's final appearance, Salisbury's role is taken up by Talbot's son, and the splittings of the death drive are recast in the form of a filial doubling: "No more can I be severed from your side," young John Talbot says, "Than can yourself yourself in twain divide" (4.5.48–49). The father dies addressing—apostrophizing—the son who lies "inhearsed in his arms" (4.7.45). Hallucinatory misreading is replaced now by a knowing imputation, and the violent torsion of the death drive toward political bellicosity is converted to a plangently sublimating redirection of revenge back against death itself:

> Talbot: Brave Death by speaking, whether he will or no;
> Imagine him a Frenchman, and thy foe.
> Poor boy, he smiles, methinks, as who should say,
> Had death been French, then Death had died to-day.
> (4.7.25–28)

The radical equivocations of the opening scene are revised now as familiar oedipal ambiguities: "I have what I would have, / Now my old arms are young John Talbot's grave" (4.7.31–32).

## 2

More than a mimetic representation, then, the scene of Talbot's first appearance actively constitutes identity and narrative trajectory out of theater's unbounded returns. In that sense, the scene could be seen to play out in starkly political terms the stammering advent of a Shakespearean, and distinctly modern, character-based dramaturgy. But it is not just the figure on stage that is constituted in the refusal of the fatal solicitation on the turret top. To the extent that the entire scene is volatilized by the threat of the viewer's subversion, it also enacts the founding of a political and sexual subjectivity beyond the stage, structured from its beginning under the aegis of a nationalist destiny and staked against the excluded and flamboyantly demonized woman.[11]

The subjectivity thus formed remains an explicitly economic one. Talbot's formative drama first emerged from the market in his opening narrative of captivity, and it is to the market that it returns. Talbot's "revenge" is completed when, a few scenes later, having recovered Orleans, he places Salisbury's body on display at precisely the point of his original, theatrical shame:

> Bring forth the body of old Salisbury,
> And here advance it in the market-place,

The middle centure of this cursed town.
Now have I paid my vow unto his soul. (2.2.4–7)

Accomplished revenge serves the more critical function of revision, as the surrogate is inscribed—literally in the epitaph Talbot composes— at the source. The aim (and the instability) of that revisionary gesture is apparent in the way that eulogy ambiguously mixes with confession and the dead assumes the characteristics of the memorialist in the inscription Talbot proposes:

> And that hereafter ages may behold
> What ruin happened in revenge of him,
> Within their chiefest temple I'll erect
> A tomb, wherein his corpse shall be interr'd
> Upon the which, that every one may read,
> Shall be engrav'd the sack of Orleance,
> The treacherous manner of his mournful death,
> And what a terror he had been to France. (2.2.10–17)

Whose "treachery" is being marked and allayed in this epitaph? Indeed, who is buried here, Salisbury, or Talbot, the true "terror of the French"? Burial here is equally a process of psychic encryption—the founding of a permanent partition within.

The burial ceremony marks a final settling of accounts, a ritualized management of the fatal appeal and impossible exchange that conditioned Talbot's emergence. The sealing off of that psychic risk coincides with the explicit convergence of the marketplace and the place of the stage—the theater the audience sees before it; theater "acknowledges" itself. The audience may acknowledge itself as well. Unsure as yet where the ebb of battle has left them, it would be difficult for theatergoers not to hear in Talbot's call to process "here, in the market place, / the middle centure of this cursed town" a reference to the present site of their viewing and to their own conditions as economic, and shamefully theatrical, beings.[12]

The hero's conquest of the martial witch fulfills the conditions for the emergence of an explicitly theatrical and economic—a commodified—subjectivity in all its blazoned and energizing shame. But it also suggests the disavowal that underwrites that construction: the marketplace intersects with the stage in the process of subject formation, but as the site of an ambiguous burial. In his introduction to the work of French psychoanalysts Nicolas Abraham and Maria Torok, Jacques Derrida writes of a tomb or "cryptic enclave" erected in the midst of the city forum or marketplace, a fragile and irreducible enclosure that defines the open space of discursive and economic circulation. "Within this forum, a place where the free circulation and exchange of objects and speeches can occur, the crypt constructs another, more inward forum like a closed rostrum or speaker's box, a *safe:* sealed, and thus internal to itself, a secret interior within the public square, but by the same token outside it, external to the interior."[13] Talbot's indeterminate ceremony, at once commemoration and repudiation, repeats in the narrative register the contradictions of this parietal, self-divided space and might be seen to allegorize the distinctive condition — the internal fault line — of a subjectivity forged from the traces of the theater and the market.

It is not commodification that inspires dread, then, however much that fate is trumpeted as the sign of a fallen age, for instance in the moralized spectacle of a king who reduces his kingdom to "rotten parchment bonds" — "live in thy shame, but die not shame with thee" — or in the spectacle of a Prince who exchanges honors and accounts with a "factor" as easily as an actor changes roles.[14] The more unsettling prospect is that the logic of exchange might by its very nature exceed any recognizable economy of self-interest, of investment and return. The scene on the turret top is striking precisely because it figures the death drive — subjectivity's insupportable limit — as a coherent and impossible completion of accounts, the rounding out of a circuit of exchange. The scene raises the possibility that revenge — that motif through which a mercantilist age figured to itself in a mode of savored reprobation its reciprocal and economistic notion of identity — might be impelled by a far more disquieting lure than aggression.[15] The repeatedly condemned and reinforced association between theater and market quells that threat at the core of Renaissance subjectivity. On the one hand, theatrical representation is bound to a localized, and thus restricted and comprehensible, version of the economic—to the *place* of the market. On the other hand, economic exchange is bound to theater's more manageable specular threat, not the death drive but a familiar, even bracing, economy of exposure and shame. To feel the depleting shame of spectacle and to know one's place in the market's speculative returns is already to have entered the space of a newly valorized and contained subjectivity.[16]

It is not coincidence, then, that the era of the market was also the era of spectacle.[17] But to speak of this simply as a historical moment overlooks how complexly history is at issue in that conjunction. In the scene of Salisbury's burial, the "encrypting" that opens the possibility of a coherent space of exchange and thus conditions the emergence of a specifically economic, speculative subject also underwrites the epitaphic discourse of history. Since its beginnings in the sixteenth century, historiography has entailed just such a paradoxical form of encryption, Michel de Certeau argues. While constituting itself against an excluded other and sustained by death's caesura, historiography simultaneously defined itself in its capacity to recover what it foreclosed: "It is an odd procedure that posits death, a breakage everywhere reiterated in discourse, and that yet denies loss by appropriating to the present the privilege of recapitulating the past as a form of knowledge."[18]

That structure of constitutive recovery—the paradoxical ellipsis of historiographic discourse per se—is inseparable from a more specific transition in representational modes. As Wlad Godzich argues, the modern concept of history emerges at the ambiguous intersection between heroic history, history as exemplum—strictly speaking, an ontological category—and history as a specifically temporal structure of legitimation. In an early modern historical discourse "that is only beginning to disengage itself from the heroic mode of history," "the ontological and the temporal are so intertwined as to be subject to confusion. This confusion is precisely what makes possible the claim that a foundational ground that is originary is recovered at some ulterior point in time."[19] The inscription of the purely ontological concept of foundation within a temporal account of recovery and return

—what is for us the virtually unquestioned structure of "history" as such—is thus a function of a distinctly early modern figural equivocation.

As the point where the heroic act becomes the very scripting, or rescripting, of the origins of the history within which the hero is inscribed—the origins of his history, the origins of the Histories—Talbot's epitaph suggests how that formative and ambiguous crossing between the exemplary and the historical is enacted around a structure of encrypting return. As if assuming from within the tragedy the role of the "fatal hand / That hath contriv'd this woeful tragedy," Talbot fulfills his heroic task by inscribing an epitaph "that hereafter ages may behold" the events we are now seeing. The hard-won funeral clearly answers to the broken ceremony that fails to stabilize the opening of the play and the Histories—it is only now that that originating act is managed. Thus the spectral nature of the burial—it is a phantasm that is being laid to rest—is mimed in the contradictory status of the eulogy, which amounts to a founding revision, and of the discourse of the play itself, which assumes its potency here by reflexively echoing and conjuring its own emptiness, like a theatrical beckoning from beyond the grave. Talbot is conjured up in all his immediacy and veracity precisely by virtue of the belatedness of the epitaph he speaks; he "emerges" to the extent that he is felt to have been what we have known him to be from the outset—a revenant. That purely discursive effect can assume the status of a historiographic founding only by virtue of the contradiction that it somehow remain a function of the exemplary, heroic act. Indeed, what's heroic here is the impossible passage from exemplum into history.

To recall Pucelle's role in the logic of the scene is to be aware of how deeply gender and sexuality are bound up with these founding mechanisms of theatrical and historical knowledge. Later in his career, at a point well beyond such unstable advents, Shakespeare stages a comparable instance of historical conjury, now with a woman—a "witch" of sorts—as its stake: Cleopatra anticipates the prospect of her capture by the Romans in terms that again vividly and uncannily foresee the present viewer's gaze.

> Mechanic slaves
> With greasy aprons, rules, and hammers shall
> Uplift us to the view . . . . . . . .
> . . . . . . . The quick comedians
> Extemporally will stage us . . . . . .
> . . . . . . . . . and I shall see
> Some squeaking Cleopatra boy my greatness. (5.2.209–220)

The paradox again here is that the historicity of the character is never more directly felt than at this moment in which the fictitious character outstrips herself: historicity "appears" in that transgression of history's expected ratio and distance. And again, the effect is explicitly intertwined with the galvanizing properties of theatrical and class shame: Cleopatra's shame at the prospect of being put on display by "mechanic slaves"; the audience's at being caught out, at having its shaming gaze returned.

The overtness of the theatrical conjury here and the overtness with which the death drive is figured as the path out of the economies of display that sustain such an effect may be functions of the fact that it is now a woman—and a demonic one at that—who is being staged. At the same time, the relatively unproblematic heroization of the "demonic" woman in the play and the relatively sublimated character of the rivening force of the scene (for the audience, theatrical self-division in this instance translates into an internalized, ethical self-contradiction, an identificatory desire that the character elude one's own mastering gaze) can be taken as measures of how thoroughly Shakespeare's entire gendered and characterological drama has established itself against the more extravagant foreclosures that marked its volatile beginnings. For all her subversiveness, Cleopatra too may be a derivative of that violent political, sexual, and representational negotiation. This would also suggest that questions of sexuality, and female sexuality in particular, should be posed not just at the level of characters and motives but in relation to the force entailed in the bringing into being of Shakespeare's distinctively character-based and "naturalistic" representation.

Any effort to historicize Talbot's drama is at least complicated, then, by the possibility that the scene structures the terms for our own distinctly modern mode of historical accounting. Does "historicizing" historicism as a mode of legitimation vitiate what claims one would want to make for the cultural and political specificity of Shakespeare's drama? One can argue that the political dimension of the subject only becomes apparent at the point where history's lapses and disjunctures come into view. Spectacle and market, subjectivity and history converge in *Henry VI* not as explanatory givens but as contingent phenomena actively constituted around their own volatile and mutually implicated limits. It would be misleading to claim that subjectivity is a function of the economic domain, that the economic is a function of history, or even that the subject is constituted within history. The scene suggests instead that subjectivity appears at the knotted limit of an entire array of discursive forms—theater, economy, history— a point of radically failed closure figured in this instance under the sign of the demonic. To acknowledge that subjectivity does not in any simple sense arise "within" history, as if history were nothing more than its transparent envelope, is to recognize that subjectivity and history are political phenomena, that is, irreducibly contingent and thus from the outset originating in an arbitrary, exclusionary, and unstable gesture of force.[20]

To realize its significance, then, one should perhaps look beyond the moment of Talbot's emergence and consider his striking returns. The earliest account of a Shakespeare production—a passage in Thomas Nashe's defense of theater—involves the return of a long-dead phantom:

Nay, what if I prove playes to be no extreame, but a rare exercise of vertue? First, for the subject of them . . . it is borrowed out of our English chronicles, wherein our forefathers valiant actes (that have lyne long buried in rustie brass and worme-eaten bookes) are revived, and they themselves raysed from the grave of oblivion, and brought to pleade their aged honours in open presence; than which, what can bee a sharper reproofe to these degenerate effeminate dayes of ours? How would it have joy'd brave Talbot (the terror of the French) to thinke that after he had lyne two hundred yeare in his tomb, he should triumph againe on the stage, and have his bones new embalmed with the teares of ten thousand spectators at least, (at severall times) who, in the tragedian that represents his person, imagine they behold him fresh bleeding?[21]

"Talbot, my life, my joy, again return'd"? While Nashe stakes the revivifying power of the stage explicitly against the usurious age's debased, indiscriminate method of making a man "spr[i]ng up," one is nevertheless struck by just how excessive Talbot's return remains in the theatrical apologist's account.[22] The hero, who returns from the "rustie brass" of the grave as if of his own accord, only to bleed freshly, recalls the equivocal opening of the Histories, where the sovereign threatens to "burst his lead and rise from death" in order to "yield the ghost." Staking theater and chronicle against the market merely brings into view that form of reiteration that exceeds and underwrites both.

There is undoubtedly an element of subversive fantasy in the account of ten thousand spectators come to see England's national hero "fresh bleeding." Pity mingles uneasily with animus in the impulse to "new embalm" the returning dead with tears. However, the fact that Nashe is drawn to the ambiguous scene of Talbot's return as the exemplum of the "vertues" of the stage suggests a more essential relationship between theater's power and these lurid signs. In a later era, literature's hold will derive from the richly complicitous prospects of narcissistic aggrandizement and apprehension in the sinuous workings of a novelistic form in which the correspondence between narrative and private historicity went without saying.[23] Here, in the era of spectacle and of a subjectivity bound less by established resources of narrativity and inwardness than by an as yet fragilely managed circuitry of exchange, the emergence of the subject is conditioned from the outset by history's proximity to the crypt, representation's proximity to demonic return, and all the possibilities of aggressive reversal and captivation implicit in theater's solicitous appeal.

# Chapter 2

# Froth in the Mirror: Demonism, Sexuality, and

# the Early Modern Subject

Few early modern phenomena call for historical analysis so imperiously as the array of beliefs and practices loosely gathered under the thrilling sign of "demonism": possession and exorcism, the satanic contract, the witch's mute and inscribing marks, necromancy, and the riveting effects of the witch's gaze. Witchcraft obviously brings into focus the social and symbolic function of gender during the era, as much of the recent work on the subject has shown. Further, because of its very strangeness, demonism is an especially rich and obvious terrain for exploring the transition between one episteme and another, for marking the advent of a modern era. In general, how better discern a culture than looking to the phenomena that occupy its margins? Although I will take up all these issues and vantage points, what interests me most is what remains after the legitimate, historicizing justifications for exploring the demonic have been exhausted, that is, fascination: the slightly prurient investment this material mobilizes, a captivation tinged with shame for anyone for whom the injunction "always historicize" has assumed axiomatic proportions.

In fact, historical analysis should not and cannot extricate itself from that remainder. Consider the way in which Greenblatt—the prime mover of Renaissance New Historicism—figures his own perhaps mildly untoward historicizing investments: "I began with the desire to speak with the dead."[1] What happens when historical analysis, with its scrupulous attention to the voice coming from elsewhere, encounters a phenomenon—demonic possession—that seems to return to it nothing more than the image of its own ventriloquizing?

Lacanians before the fact, conjurers themselves knew that invoking the dead was largely a matter of receiving one's own message in inverted form.[2] And yet, historical analysis may never be closer to its legitimating sources than it is at this point, where its relation to the past assumes the form of a solicitation at once familiar and strange, the point of fascination.

In what follows, I tease out fascination, as an element of demonism but also as that which comes into view just where demonism becomes problematic as an object of analysis, even as an objective social phenomenon, and trace its significance well beyond the arcane practices of witches. Understood in its technical acceptation as the scotomizing effect of the witch's gaze, "fascination" reveals the fundamental relationship between witchcraft as a social formation and the erotic lineaments of the early modern subject. Such a gaze affords particularly promising grounds for exploring the horizon of the modern subject and its relation to a distinct, emerging social/symbolic order. At the same time, part of my broader methodological aim in focusing on witchcraft is to complicate what has become the stark, tendentiously ordering divide in Renaissance studies between historicism—especially the empirical "history from below" within whose terms the witchcraft phenomenon has generally been considered—and "high" philosophy or theory. This means discovering the historically contingent taint of the witch's gaze within the pure space and time of the Cartesian subject, and thus, perhaps, the modern psychoanalytic subject as well. But it can also involve taking into account the ways in which this particular analytical "object" brings to view the condition and limits of the project of empirical history generally.

That methodological aim—troubling the boundaries between high and low—in part explains the slightly extravagant trajectory of the analysis that follows as it moves from a sociological account of the occult practices of witches to a reading of one of the era's famous aesthetic articulations of the contours of the human subject: Michelangelo's *Last Judgment*. Obviously, the transnational character of such an analysis, the passage it enacts from Protestant England to Counter-Reformation Italy, flies in the face of more finely shaded cultural and materialist histories. One could, I think, offer a persuasive historical narrative of the relation between the forms of consolidating social abjection operative in the one cultural context and the flamboyantly private self-exorcism at work in the other. At the same time, it would be a mistake, I think, to treat the aesthetic merely as an element within such a cultural/historical narrative. Michelangelo's eschatological work is about the conditions of history as such, and to find the subject figured there in explicitly demonic form precisely as the material remainder of the passage into history is to say something about the problematic nature of the relations among subjectivity, materiality, and history in the early modern era.

I

As a social formation, witchcraft can hardly be said to have resisted analysis. If anything, it has been too yielding. In addition to considering Greenblatt's analysis of exorcism, which proceeds in terms of the political and institutional opposition between an Anglican orthodoxy and a religious minority seeking to legitimize itself through marginal charismatic practices, one might take into account the broader, anthropologically inflected accounts of scholars such as Alan Macfarlane and Keith Thomas, who conceive the phenomenon, at least in its English manifestation, in terms of the erosion of a feudal network of social bonds on the one hand and the decline of religion as a magically instrumental practice on the other; one might also turn to the structural accounts of critics such as Catherine Belsey, Peter Stallybrass, and Karen Newman, who associate the craze with efforts to contain the threat of female transgression as it was experienced during the crisis of order in the early modern era.[3] Together, these accounts tend to confirm a generalized relation between the demonic and historical crisis. But the awkwardness increases as one attempts to concatenate them with any measure of precision, a project that finds one locating the witchcraft threat at once with the figure possessed and the charismatic exorcist, and seeing the witch herself as both a figure of social transgression and the representative of traditional communal bonds, as harbinger of formations to come and ghost of formations past.

40

The problem of locating witchcraft is not a recent one. Witchcraft tracts themselves are constantly and vividly unclear about where, exactly, the threat is coming from. Here is John Cotta on necromantic impostors:

> Lastly, may be collected and observed, the use and necessity of distinction between Imposture and Witchcraft; namely, that the odious and abominable sinne of witchcraft be not suffered to continue unregarded and neglected under the color of vaine Imposture, and that the Devill be not suffered to live amongst us too commonly and too openly in the coat and habite of the foolish Impostor or Juggler. For certainely, nothing doth more hood-winke the through-discovery of Sorcerers, then remissenesse and omission of inquisition and castigation of Impostors, out of whose leaven (no doubt) but diligent animadversion, might oft-times boult many a subtill and concealed witch.[4]

Although Cotta begins by speaking of the "necessity and use of distinction," the problem is that there may be no clear distinction between witchcraft and imposture. If anything, the impostor is more dangerous, for in him the devil has found a way to conceal himself openly, to remain all the more hidden for the transparency of the ruse.

Cotta's claim is a variant of the more common argument that the exorcist accomplishes the devil's work. "The devil pretends to be compelled the more slyly to delude," writes Johann Weyer: "Truly these exorcists should fittingly be classed with the enchanters."[5] According to George Gifford and other Anglican apologists, those who seek out the cure for witchcraft in soothsayers and cunning men are all the more seduced by the devil. The devil feigns his expulsion "and so entereth deeper"; he "lets go his hold" only to "taketh faster holde."[6] Such arguments reflect the potentially labyrinthine paradoxes of an institutional authority that felt compelled to invoke the devil to debunk the exorcists and their galvanizing practices.[7] They may also be read in light of a larger cultural movement of sublimation that shifts the invested locus of scrutiny inward, making the demonic a function of beliefs rather than of possessing spirits.[8] But neither account acknowledges what is most remarkable about the accusation. When

Gifford suggests that the devil is conjured by his expulsion—that he goes farther in by being cast out—he articulates the logic of possession in its purest form: as a force that inhabits all the more for being foreclosed, that magically bypasses the most resilient limits.

While an exorcist could be a conjurer, the witch herself tended to be most visible in her curative function. "When a supposed witch . . . doth touch [the bewitched] . . . he or she immediately are delivered from the present fit or agonie, that then was upon him or her."[9] Indeed, the witch need only enter the room for all symptoms to unknit themselves, as Mother Samuel discovered to her ruin: "In what kind of extremity soever these children were in . . . so soon as ever she had set foot into the parlour or hall where they were, they would all presently start up upon their feet and be as well as any in the house, and so continue while she was present."[10] The restorative effects of the witch's presence can lead to some striking expedients; in the Warboys case, the children moved in with the witch.[11] Such reversals extend to the most intimate mechanisms of possession. Surprisingly, no one ever seems surprised that it is the possessing demon who exposes the witch, a penchant for self-betrayal that more than any other fact suggests possession's exact equivalence in the hysterical symptom.[12]

All these elisions between expulsion and conjury, between threat and cure, simply confirm what is abundantly obvious about witchcraft—that it is nothing if not a transferential phenomenon. Luridly so, sometimes. Here's an account of the victimization by witchcraft of Lord Strange, perhaps not coincidentally the patron of Shakespeare's company:

> A homely woman, about the age of 50 years, was found mumbling in a corner of his Honour's chamber, but what, God knoweth. This wise woman (as they termed her) seemed often to ease his Honour both of his vomiting and hiccock; but so it fell out, which was strange, that when so long as he was eased, the woman herself was troubled most vehemently in the same manner, the matter which she vomiting being like also that which passed from him.[13]

Strange indeed, particularly in this context, to be speaking of what "fell out." More often, the scene of witchcraft is transferential in a purer, strictly epistemological sense. "Persons bewitched shall in the time of their strange fits or trances nominate or accuse a witch, and for a true testimony against him or her, thus nominated shall reveale . . . the very words or works which the supposed or thus nominated witch shall be acting or speaking in farre distant places, even in the very moment and point of time while they are in acting or speaking."[14] The synchronism of the marvel is critical, for the mystery of witchcraft is less a matter of prophetic knowledge than of a knowledge spoken from elsewhere, from another scene.

It is the transferential nature of demonic possession that has lent the phenomenon to psychoanalytic accounts. What has not been recognized is the extent to which this very ungroundedness lies at the core of witchcraft's status as a social formation. Consider a contradiction informing modern efforts to read witchcraft socially: Most analyses, particularly feminist analyses, have argued that witch beliefs should be understood in terms of a logic of social exclusion; demonization, prompted by the crisis of order in early modern Europe, amounts to a concerted suppression and containment of the unruly woman, especially the woman subversive of gender structures.[15] Other accounts, however, specifically distinguish witch belief from the mechanics of scapegoating. Unlike the contemporaneous social exclusion of the Jew or the Catholic in England, Thomas argues, the demonization of the witch involves an individual dynamic of guilt and projection.[16] The victim of bewitchment turns out in most instances to have initiated the antagonism by slighting the witch, refusing her appeal for charity. The resulting sense of guilt is at once realized in the form of the symptom and repudiated in the demonization of the witch. Thomas associates that dynamic with the psychic turmoil prompted by the breakdown of feudal structures of community and customary tenancies during the early modern era. For Thomas, then, the witch embodies rather than threatens traditional symbolic community; rather than consolidating an imperiled social totality, demonization amounts to a psychic negotiation that preserves the individual subject outside a traditional network of bonds.[17]

Everything we have seen about witchcraft encourages us not to resolve these contradictory readings. Is the witch the figure whose repudiation breaches or affirms the symbolic network? She is demonic to the extent that she abolishes the distinction between those gestures, between exorcism and conjury, between casting out and constituting, and thus exposes the limit of society itself understood as a coherent or objectifiable totality. If witchcraft seems an extravagantly overdetermined instance of social friction — between a patriarchal order and the transgressive woman, between a religious orthodoxy and the marginal charismatic practices of Puritans and Catholics, between nascent capitalism and a receding feudal order — it is because it represents such antagonism as a function of overdetermination itself, the fact that even the most hegemonic, the most "real," of social or symbolic formations remains incapable of totalizing itself and thus of constituting itself in objective form. A *crimen exceptum* (a crime consisting entirely in its being labeled as such) among positively defined transgressions, the demonic is also the exception that exposes the apparitional nature of the entire social domain and the phenomenal forms that make it up.[18] To use the language of the political theorists Ernesto Laclau and Chantal Mouffe, the demonic amounts to that point within the social body, as well as within the body of the possessed, where "negativity as such" takes on a "real existence."[19]

That association between the possessed body and the overdetermined, which is to say, symbolic character of society itself is evident at the most intimate level of the drama of possession. What better figure for the "floating signifier," the signifier in excess of the subject it animates, than the era's endlessly invoked spectacle of lips moving out of synch with the voice?[20] The overdetermined effects of the symbolic are no less evident in the tireless accounts of the body inscribed: the betraying marks on the body of the witch or the bewitched, the "little scroll . . . espied to be hidden betweene [the] skin and flesh" of the witch who would not burn.[21]

The association between witchcraft and symbolic inscription suggests the unspoken subtext of the new, uniquely early modern preoccupation with the satanic compact; a play like Christopher Marlowe's *Dr. Faustus*, for instance, may be less interested in deals with devils than it is with what is demonic about the nature of contract as such: the possibility that the subject might ascribe to an arbitrary rep-

44

resentational structure that extends beyond that subject's own limit and demise.[22] Even the model of discretionary subjection associated with contract theory, however, may function to temper other, less localizable anxieties related to the effects of inscription. To understand why a king who came to fancy himself a political theorist of stature should have begun with a tract on demonology, we need to hear in his account of the "intolerable dolour that [witches] feele in that place where [the devil] has marked her" something of the melancholy loss that conditions the advent of every subject within the political/symbolic field.[23]

Understood thus, the scene of possession would seem at once to bear out and to problematize arguments for a direct relation between the witch epidemic and the emergence of the state. For Robert Muchembled, the European witch-hunt tells "the universal story of the advance of public authority against particularism," the story of how the state, conceived as a centralized and abstract embodiment of law, realizes itself by at once absorbing and abolishing particularized and discrete instances of communal belief and justice. But if demonism marks such an advent, it does so only insofar as it embodies a contradiction inherent in the law, a contradiction that troubles the distinction between law's universality and the particularities against which it acts, between the law and its effects. The paradoxical fact of having, in Muchembled's words, to "appeal to the law for protection against the dangers it has itself conjured up" describes the essential condition of the law, what makes its relation to demonism irreducible.[24]

The relation between demonic possession and law does not in itself explain fascination, however; nor does it even suggest what is unique about witchcraft. For witchcraft is not the only site within the early modern political anatomy where the symbolic—negativity "as such" —assumes privileged visibility. What is the relation between the body of the bewitched and that other double body, the king's? The king, too, is someone possessed, inhabited by another body—the body politic. He is even an inherently exorbitant figure, for at least according to monarchic ideology in its purest form, the sovereign is most truly present in his demise. What is that magical surplus, the true and invisible mark of sovereignty, but, again, the hypostatized embodiment

45

of the symbolic as such, what remains of the social field in and beyond the subjects who make it up?[25]

But a witch is not a king. At opposite ends of the political anatomy, the two are nonetheless asymmetrical. The king manifests the symbolic in its pure form as a function of negation. "The king is a thing . . . of nothing," Hamlet says. The king is an equivocal being, absolute, empty: absolute to the extent that he is empty, for above all he manifests "the paradox of identification with nonidentity, with the gap that maintains desire" within the symbolic order.[26] The possessing demon is also nothing—"no nature of its own," King James says—and yet, insistently, a thing, "the thing," as the enchanted children (Heideggerians all) persist in calling it during the Warboys trial.[27] While both the sovereign and the witch embody the symbolic function—the surplus of sign over being—the witch also entails what remains of the body, especially the maternal body, in excess of the symbolic network as a whole.[28]

If the sovereign—man or woman—is phallic, the very embodiment of division in its constitutive relation to desire, the witch is manifestly a part-object or, in the Lacanian schema, an *objet petit a* (object small a). To enlist a witch's power, one needs "some part or parcell of garments, or any excrements belonging unto them, as their hayre" or "nail pairings."[29] The forms can be multiplied indefinitely, for their power lies not in themselves but in their status as residue, that is, what is of the subject yet beyond the subject, internal yet alien and intractable. In that sense, a sign more precise even than the oddly migratory "teat" on the witch's body is the visceral and intangible wound King James describes: "a marke upon some secret place of their bodie, which remains soore unhealed . . . and thereafter ever insensible, howsoever it be nipped or pricked by any."[30]

The witch broaches not just symbolic negation but also that which has been forcibly jettisoned in order for negation to coalesce in a specular, identificatory form and thus for the symbolic in all its elusive, reverting effects to appear as a function at all.[31] If the demonic makes something visible, it does so in a form that is not reducible to the specular relation that gives identity its form and contour. The *objet petit a*, Lacan tells us, has by definition no specular image. The witch,

46

Reginald Scot tells us, "leaves in a looking glasse a certeine froth."[32] And yet, what cannot be assimilated to the specular, identificatory relation also cannot be purged from it: that is where the threat lies and where the fascination begins.

After his encyclopedic debunking of demonological practices (literally after the chapter entitled "A conclusion against witchcraft"), Scot acknowledges that something remains unexplained: fascination, fascination in the technical sense of the witch's power to possess and subvert with her gaze. To explain the contagious effects of the witch's look, Scot resorts to "natural magic" and humoral theory. He may have been closer to the mark earlier, when he noted a contradiction in the mythology of bewitchment. "Item: the examiner [in a judicial inquest] must looke stedfastlie upon their eies, for they cannot looke directlie upon a man's face (as Bodin affirmeth in one place, although in another he saith, that they kill and destroie both men and beasts with their lookes.)"[33] To solve the riddle and recognize its bearing on specular captivation, one must read witchcraft as an embodiment of the problematic of self-relation. The witch cannot look at one when one looks directly at her, any more than one could see oneself seeing oneself. And yet, because one only comes into sight dialectically — by seeing oneself see — to see at all is to feel oneself from the outset subject to and inscribed within an alien gaze, one's own seeing as it derives from elsewhere.[34]

Such captivation is not merely a reversal of positions in the dialectics of specular identification. Instead, it is a reflexive inversion that subverts the relation between sight and visibility. In an etching from George Bartisan's *Opthalmologeia* that shows the effects of fascination, the eye of the bewitched subject is not simply obtruded or objectified but turned back in on itself, eluding in its movement the difference between seeing and being seen (fig. 1). In that sense, the image represents with considerable precision the "underside of consciousness" in what Lacan calls the "inside-out structure of the gaze," sight as it constitutes itself around an originating division and inversion.[35] In the gaze, sight itself, the locus of being, assumes the alien, internal form of the demonic wound. The significance of this instance of ocular fascination becomes apparent when one views it historically. Under

Figure 1. Example of ocular fascination.
Etching in Georges Bartisan, *Opthalmologeia*
(Dresden, 1583).

the heading of pathology, at the farthest reaches of the demonic, the image reveals the unacknowledged ground of a reflexive subject whose illusory autonomy will be founded on its claim to see itself see.[36]

2

Understood structurally, then, witchcraft is not so much an instance of social banishment as it is the arbitrary and enforced exclusion that constitutes and ceaselessly de-realizes society as such, as a phenomenal field. The "embodied," literalized character of that limit can be seen to be proportionate to the "organic," totalized character of the body politic such a figure structures and haunts. At the same time, the unseen taint of witchcraft bears no less directly on the sexual contours of the early modern subject, a conjunction that bears out the claim that subjectivity is less a social construct than it is a function of the insistent failure of society to constitute itself.

To the extent that it exposes reflexive sight as a self-divided sight, Bartisan's image of possession shows speculative, ratiocinative subjectivity to be a function of castration and desire—to be a sexual phenomenon. And yet, fascination may also draw one beyond that familiar construction of the sexual function oriented around a threatening lack. The pop-eyed grotesque would have suggested sexuality more directly than one might imagine, for not just sight but sex itself was considered a reversible phenomenon during the era. According to early modern anatomical theory and popular belief, there was only one sex, the male sex, the female genitalia consisting of an inside-out version of the male's. In principle at least, sex could reverse itself at any moment.[37]

It is difficult not to read such radical isomorphism as a concerted suppression of the function of division and difference in sexuality, that is, entirely in relation to castration anxiety. The very thoroughness of the exclusion should give us pause, however. In a later age, sexual lack will be hypostatized in and fear structured around the figure of the "castrated" woman. Here, where difference seems to be at once foreclosed altogether and gathered into a single, seamless movement of

49

turning around, the threat that is summoned is not so much castration as the more paradoxical loss of loss. In the very tightness of its specular inversions, the early modern sexual system seems to resonate directly with a domain beyond the symbolic register and the lack that ostentatiously structures it.[38]

To bear out such intuitions about the distinctive contours of early modern identity, one must return to the gaze, tracing it beyond witchcraft to its recurrences within the scientific and aesthetic domains of the era, beginning with its relation to the emergence of a new mode of apprehending the human body. As Thomas Laqueur points out, the earliest Renaissance anatomical texts that turned away from a reliance on classical authorities were in fact more invested in the theatricalized gesture of displaying than in any naturalistic representation of the body displayed.[39] This preoccupation with display is evident in an interesting surplus of sight in relation to the object seen, as intimated by the frequency with which frontispieces to anatomical textbooks present the entire anatomical theater to our gaze and by the eroticized emptiness around which the most famous of the anatomical scenes, Andreas Vesalius's *De Humani Corporis*, is structured: at its center, as it turns out, Vesalius's theater triumphantly displays the hollow womb of a convict who had sought to avoid execution by claiming pregnancy—literally a hysterical display (fig. 2).[40]

As Patricia Parker has shown, anatomical texts of the early modern era consistently orient themselves around the spectacle of the woman's body "dilated" and laid open to view, a scene at once empowering for the masculine scientific gaze and, in Helkiah Crooke's words, "too obscoene to look upon."[41] The threat, as well as the reassurance, in that violent laying bare is suggested by the implicit reflexiveness of the act. The slit open bodies seem to offer back not just a vaginal figure but an image of the viewer's own eye (fig. 3); the implied possibility of autodissective rending is realized in the persistent and odd motif of the self-anatomizing corpse (fig. 4).[42]

But the historic significance of such self-dissecting images runs deeper. Consider the well-known illustration to Juan de Valverdi's treatise, *Anatomia del Corporo Humano* (fig. 5). A classically posed figure displays his precisely rendered and labeled musculature while

ANDREAE VESALII
BRVXELLENSIS, SCHOLÆ
medicorum Patauinæ profeſſoris, de
Humani corporis fabrica
Libri ſeptem.

CVM CAESAREAE
Maieſt. Galliarumq; Regis, ac Senatus Veneti gra-
tia & priuilegio, ut in diplomatis eorundem continetur.

BASILEÆ.

Figure 2. Frontispiece, Andreas Vesalius, *De Humani Corporis* (Basil, 1543).
Courtesy of the Chapin Library of Rare Books, Williams College, MA.

Figure 3. Frontispiece, in Andreas Vesalius, *De Humani Corporis*
(Amsterdam, 1642). Courtesy of the Wangensteen Historical Library of
Biology and Medicine, University of Minnesota.

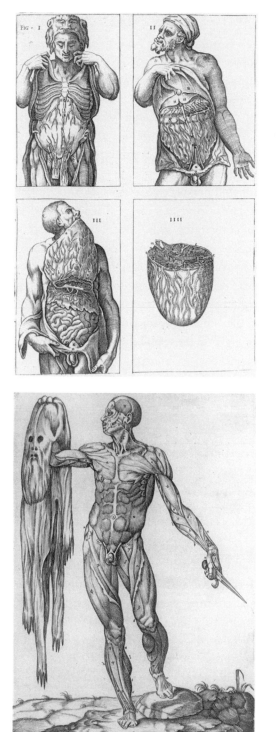

Figure 4. Self-anatomizing corpses. Etching in Juan de Valverdi, *Anatomia del Corporo Humano* (Rome, 1560). Courtesy of the Chapin Library of Rare Books, Williams College, MA.

*(below)* Figure 5. Figure holding its own flayed skin. Etching in de Valverdi, *Anatomia del Corporo Humano* (Rome, 1560). Courtesy of the Chapin Library of Rare Books, Williams College, MA.

holding up for his gaze as well as ours his own flayed skin, the inside-out leftover of his body proper. Devon Hodges associates that sort of unseemly detritus, strikingly common in anatomical images of the period, with the violence implicit in the newly emerging process of scientific objectification itself.[43] To see how much the gaze is at stake in that anatomizing process, however, one must view the reversed, attenuated apparition that clings to the figure in more precise terms as something of a natural anamorphic image.

Lacan associates those distorted perspective images with the faltering emergence of the Cartesian subject, a subject that amounted to the unitary reference point of converging sight lines. The anamorphic image betrayed the real sources of scopic pleasure precisely in the veering off from such a geometric grid, a torsion of sight experienced by the subject as a form of erotic eclipse.[44] The anatomical image suggests, then, that if something must be shed to bring forth the empirical body—the body as object of a sovereign, scientific vision—it is not just the skin but the gaze, or sight in its sexual dimension.

During the early modern era, that anamorphic skin continued to cling to even the most sovereign of viewing subjects, to judge from one of the period's truly monumental self-portraits: Michelangelo's *Last Judgment*. Obviously, one doesn't generally consider that eschatological extravaganza as an instance of portraiture, or one does so only implicitly, by reference beyond its limit to the vision of the figure who imagined it. Yet, as scholars now agree, Michelangelo does appear there in the midst of the furious action, inscribed in cryptic form in the flayed and stretched skin that the martyr St. Bartholomew holds toward us (fig. 6).

That mysterious form is hardly marginal to the scene. As Leo Steinberg points out, the clandestine self-portrait gains prominence by virtue of falling at the exact midpoint of the painting's strongest formal feature, a diagonal running from the cross and crown of thorns borne aloft in the upper left lunette, down through the wound in Christ's side, through the flayed skin, through the solitary and conscience-stricken sinner with his hand covering one eye, and finally to the figure of a serpent-encircled prince of darkness, the most prominent of the demons, at the lower right corner of the fresco (fig. 7).

Figure 6. St. Bartholomew's skin. Detail, Michelangelo's *The Last Judgment* (Sistine Chapel, Vatican Palace, Vatican State, 1508–1512). Reproduced with permission of Scala/Art Resource.

Figure 7. Christ and St. Bartholomew. Detail, Michelangelo's *The Last Judgment* (Sistine Chapel, Vatican Palace, Vatican State, 1508–1512). Reproduced with permission of Scala/Art Resource.

"To put it literally, letting metaphor fall where it may: it is the extension of the self's axis that strings the continuum of heaven and hell."[45] Furthermore, the extended portrait falls directly beneath the all-powerful gaze of Christ in judgment, lending a profoundly subjective cast to the universal drama (fig. 8). "The whole cosmic drama . . . collapses upon a single destiny."[46] To suggest, however, that the artist appears as the object of Christ's gaze simplifies the effect: Drawn not just downward but diagonally along the line of the "judge's" sight, Michelangelo represents himself as function more than object of that sovereign gaze, an effect of Christ's own anamorphic regard.[47]

The anamorphic nature of the image clearly realizes a humility topos, testifying to the artist's abjection before divine judgment. But the distorted sight lines of the portrait would have made viewers aware of other peculiar compositional features of the painting, in particular, the way in which it averts itself from their own gaze. As de Tolnay has shown, the entire composition is oriented diagonally toward a vantage point no viewer on the chapel floor can inhabit, that is, toward the window of the chamber in the first bay of the chapel's right wall, where the pontiff was able to view the mass unseen.[48] In the portrait, the artist may thus be bringing into view his location at the annihilating point of convergence of a set of absolute and irreconcilable gazes, the sight lines of spiritual and political, private and public authority that constituted the subject position of the artist within a patronage system. Michelangelo executed the fresco under papal duress, one might recall, and spoke passionately of the attenuating effects of his patrons' manifold and simultaneous demands.[49]

But even that reading may ground the form too thoroughly. Consider another form that lurks in the skin. As William Heckscher points out, Michelangelo's face mingles with the face of a dog, as if the bodies were one or the hound bore the artist in its mouth.[50] The allusion may be a private one; during his later years, Michelangelo took to wrapping himself in the hides of dogs.[51] But the flayed skin and the hound have literary resonances as well. In canto 13 of the *Inferno*, the poet and his guide come upon the shade of a suicide who has been transformed into a bleeding tree. The ghost speaks of his fate on the occasion of the Last Judgment, articulating Dante's own re-

Figure 8. *The Last Judgment,* by Michelangelo (Sistine Chapel,
Vatican Palace, Vatican State, 1508–1512). Reproduced with permission
of Scala/Art Resource.

vision of the rule that all—the saved and the damned—will reassume their bodies at the resurrection: "Like the rest we shall go for the cast-off flesh we have left, but not so that any of us will be clothed in it again, for it is not just that one should have that of which he robs himself. We shall drag them here and through the dismal wood our bodies will be hung, each on the bush of its injurious shade." As the condemned speaks, the woods are filled with the sounds of a terrible chase. Two damned—the spendthrifts, who are suicides by virtue of their willful and self-depleting excesses—appear, naked and cowering. "Behind them the wood was full of black bitches, ravenous and swift like hounds loosed from the chain; on him that squatted there they set their teeth and tore him apart piecemeal, then carried off these suffering members."[52]

The relationship of the suicides, each with their limply hanging bodies, to Michelangelo's personal context is evident enough: What could be a more vivid confession of abjection than to liken oneself to those who remain dispossessed on the final day? But what of the hunt? The connection arises through Dante's familiar subtext, "the most famous of all myths of dismemberment and fragmentation."[53] During the early modern era, the Ovidian tale of the hunter Actaeon being turned to a hart at the sight of Diana and torn asunder by his own dogs was read both as an emblem of the reverting effects of untoward desires and as an allegory of visual transgression, the consequences of beholding the forbidden sight of political majesty, for instance.[54] The anamorphic image *as* anamorph arises precisely at the intersection of these scopic and reversionary elements, at the point where, turning upon and dividing itself, sight realizes itself solely in the elusive, "pulsatile and spread-out function" of the gaze.[55] To the extent that it thus figures sight in its radical form as divided and autonomous drive, the anamorphic skin asks the viewer to reverse the vectors of power intersecting the scene; rather than representing the artist as victim of arrayed powers, the portrait would be the locus of the drive from which every surveying power—church and state, public and private—derives.

Why should the artist's only known self-portrait appear in this painting of all paintings? Michelangelo's vast eschatological fresco represents a significant turning point in the evolution of the genre from hieratic image to recreated drama.[56] That transformation also coincides with the emergence of a subject defined as "pure power of annihilation," the power to reduce all—heaven and earth, past and future—to the visible object of its gaze.[57] That such a masterful being should include itself within the field of objects would not in itself be paradoxical. To know itself at all, the subject must enter into a dialectical oscillation between object and subject, a dialectic of loss and restoration. And yet, neither exactly a subject nor exactly an object, the anamorphic figure falls outside such dialectics of identity altogether, outside even the time of universal judgment and human history. Sole witness among the living of the end, the artist is, simultaneously, the only figure that remains unanimated after the resurrection of the living and the dead, as if by some logic the witness alone were condemned to miss the event that gives meaning to all human history. As self-portraiture, then, the *Last Judgment* realizes in an extravagantly precise form that brush with the limits of the dialectics of identity and history which Lacan calls "the encounter forever missed."[58]

To discern more precisely how that precarious, apparitional subjectivity is sustained, one must consider the self-portrait in terms of the erotic economy of the painting as a whole. The strong, organizing diagonal Steinberg traces runs from the signs of Christ's sacrifice at one extreme to a demonic figure encircled by a serpent that holds the devil's penis in its mouth (fig. 9). Although Steinberg reads that strange figure as an inverted image of marriage—"the serpent's glide adown that male torso betraying a connubial routine of fellation, the phallus received in its lodgment defining the spouse"—the striking redundancy of the erotic encounter, in which a phallus fellates a phallus, as well as the vague hermaphroditism of the devil should give us pause.[59] In fact, the figure is more immediately legible in terms of the opposition between the signifiers of redemptive loss at one pole of the fresco—the cross, the crown of thorns, the wound—and, at the other, an image of extravagant autoerotic completion, a lurid embodiment of the same-sex theory.

The demon represents the fall, then, not as a function of loss—cas-

60

Figure 9. Demonic figure. Detail, Michelangelo's *The Last Judgment*
(Sistine Chapel, Vatican Palace, Vatican State, 1508–1512). Reproduced
with permission of Scala/Art Resource.

tration's wound has redemptive force here—but, again, as a loss of loss. The human figures arrayed beneath Christ on the diagonal might be seen to embody sight fallen subject to castration in two distinct forms: as the annihilating effects of the gaze in the case of the self-portrait; as a scotomizing of sight associated with an inward, subjectivizing turn of conscience in the case of the huddled sinner. And yet that conjunction between sight and the splitting of the subject arises on the far side of castration, as it were, at a point of juncture between the symbolic domain structured around sacrifice and an impossible pleasure somewhere beyond. For the viewer, then, the threat does not inhere in the paradoxical fact that the entire dramatic vortex of the scene is organized around a site of loss: Christ's wound at the center of the fresco. The danger lies in what the eye discovers beyond the legible significations of the painting, as sight finds itself within the absorptive workings of the gaze: that loss itself is a fragile stay.

The loss of loss, the same-sex theory: all this could of course be read structurally and biographically as an explicitly homosocial staging of desire, or as an instance of what Luce Irigaray dubs the "hom(m)o-sexual" economy, an erotic economy of the self-same. But to construe the image thus is anachronistic, for it fails to recognize how the homoerotic aspects of the scene operate within the representational economies specific to the era in which it was created. The single-sex theory is only the most startling instance of the vast circuit of similitude that binds together microcosm and macrocosm during the early modern era.[60] The specularity of that system should not be construed simply as an elaborate affirmation of the (male) subject as ample and complete at the expense of symbolic and sexual difference. The insistence of the gaze implies a subject explicitly conceived as a function of a specular economy that goes beyond it, as a function of sight before it is a subject that sees. But if the gaze divides even as it constitutes, it nevertheless does so according to a logic distinct from the dialectics of symbolization. If the scopic drive of all drives "most completely eludes the term castration," that is because, never assuming the dignity or autonomy of symbolic negation, the lack the gaze inscribes appears solely as the elusive reverse-face of the specular relation itself—subjectivity's foreign and tenacious skin.[61]

That sometimes uncanny hearkening directly from the specular relation to a "beyond" of symbolization—the taint in the mirror of the early modern subject—can be understand in terms of representational epochs. Dolar suggests that we read the Enlightenment as a protracted experiment in mapping subjectivity directly onto the symbolic, an effort to conceive a purely social subject without recourse to imaginary investments.[62] The early modern, in contrast, would seem to entail a mapping of the imaginary subject directly onto the real, as if subjectivity could be formed without recourse to a dialectics of symbolization.

Such representational shifts have a political dimension, for they are bound up with the subjective transformations entailed in the emergence of the state. As capitalist relations of production and exchange supervened on the hierarchies of the feudal era and a social sphere emerged, the law conceived as a formal category also arose for the first time as the necessary pendant to a newly valorized, freely acting subject. "Because they were objective [the laws] secured a space for what was most subjective; because they were abstract, for what was most concrete."[63] The emergence of the self-constituting subject will depend on the gradual separating out of the symbolic as an inviolate category, for the very idea of the law as pure formal constraint—our idea of the law—amounts to the obverse of that autonomous subjectivity and its illusory freedom. Slavoj Žižek writes: "[The] experience of the given, non-founded character of customs and social rules entails in itself a kind of distance from them. In the traditional, pre-enlightened universe, the authority of the Law is never experienced as nonsensical and unfounded; on the contrary, the Law is always illuminated by the charismatic power of fascination."[64]

To understand the exact nature of that prior, charismatic universe, one must read "fascination" here in all its demonic specificity. After all, the sovereign, too, was capable of reversing sight and visibility with his own tangible, annihilating gaze, although the demonic grounds of such a charismatic technology must go unacknowledged. "Kings have many ears and many eyes," Erasmus tells us, "They have eyes that espy out more things than men could think."[65] Such a dispensation is characterized neither by the law as pure and arbitrary form, nor by any preoccupation with the body in its primitive, pre-symbolic organizing properties as the critical preoccupation with the carnivalesque has suggested; instead it is characterized by the far stranger possibility that the symbolic itself—negativity "as such"—might be freighted with an odd, erotic density. The exclusion of that residue will banish demons, even as it opens a new era of subjects, laws, and rights.

But to cast fascination simply as a revealing interval in the evolution of a modern subject is to lose sight of the larger insight it offers. Acknowledging the contingency, which is to say the strangeness, of fascination means recognizing what makes it problematic in relation to any symbolic dialectic, including that of narrative history. Precisely insofar as the emerging early modern subject appears where the familiar logic of symbolic negation falters, it will remain not a subject of history but history's anamorphosis, an apparitional, familiar, and strange, thing. Return to Bartisan's bewitched and reverted eye and consider what makes it an arresting figure for historicism and psychoanalysis alike: the possibility that that form is at once the origin and the effect of an alien gaze—one's own. To allow that prospect is to recognize what makes fascination fascination, that is, its power to solicit and eclipse in a single, reversionary movement. But it is also to suggest that the most authentic history, the one that avoids endless dialectical affirmation and thus avoids condemning one to find oneself everywhere one looks, is the history that rigorously situates itself at the level of the missed encounter.[66] Although psychoanalysis affords such an insight, it is also true, in this instance, that history appears where the psychoanalytic gaze tellingly misses its mark.

# Chapter 3

# Vanishing Point

Having explored the subject in its odd and anamorphic manifestations, symptoms or indices of the social/symbolic transformations of the early modern era, I now approach the subject head on, as it were, by focusing on the representational development that most directly suggests the emergence of a formal subject structured around its own negation: that is, the appearance of the pictorial vanishing point.[1] The association between that visual device and the symbolic calling into being of a subject is figured nowhere so vividly or precisely as it is in the Renaissance variants of the event that amounts to the ur-instance of subjective interpellation in western culture: the scene of the Annunciation, in which the Virgin is hailed into her sacred destiny.

To trace the lineaments of modern secular subjectivity in a genre of devotional images will seem, of course, quixotic. Indeed, to venture any connection between fifteenth-century representations of the Annunciation and the mechanism through which subjects are interpellated or inscribed within a symbolic field is arguably to risk imposing a modern and secular set of preoccupations on an alien domain. It is worth noting, less to banish than to complicate such methodological qualms, that it is precisely in its miraculous dimensions—as figuration of the Word become flesh, a message that brings into being what it announces—that the scene most obviously resonates with contemporary accounts of the performative character of symbolic inscription. To anyone schooled in modern psychoanalytic discourse, the sense of recognition can be startling; consider the way the words spoken by the angel are inscribed upside down and backward on some of these images, giving literal form to Lacan's well-known dictum that, in the field of the Other, the sender always receives her message in inverted form (fig. 10).[2] That sort of uncanny recognition—the sensation of

Figure 10. *Annunciation,* by Jan van Eyck (1432). Ghent Altar,
Cathedral St. Bavo, Ghent, Belgium. Reproduced by permission
of Giraudon/Art Resource.

being surprised by what one already knew would be the case—is, in a sense, what symbolic interpellation, in all its temporal ellipticalness, is "all about." Then again, the possibility remains that images such as these articulate the condition, and thus the legible horizon of such familiar, symbolic effects.

I argue these annunciatory images entail, paradoxically enough, an iconoclastic, negational logic particular to the form and temporality of an emerging subject; in that sense, they "announce" the subject as a subject necessarily in advance of itself, as a historical syncope. That secular and, I'll argue, intrinsically social being is fully developed in a work of a very different representational order, a drama seemingly less concerned with advents than with fallings away, less with sacred invocation than with exorcism. While *King Lear* suggests the linguistic and erotic underpinnings of the perspective effect and the emergent empirical subject associated with it, the play also reveals a phantasmatic structuring space beyond such effects, and thus beyond the negational subject, its reverse face as it were. That space—or, rather, the entire, articulating opposition between empiricism and fantasy, the vanishing point and its beyond—coincides with the emergence of a radically distinct sociality and a distinctly political subjectivity.

I

I want to begin by focusing on the most striking formal feature of Annunciation scenes as they evolved during the Renaissance, the feature that most directly suggests the emergence of something modern in their representational logic: the dramatic perspective recession that comes to interpose itself between Mary and her Angelic intercessor. The effect is evident for instance, in Domenico Veneziano's *Annunciation* from 1445 (fig. 11), perhaps the earliest use of the device; Piero della Francesca's Perugia *Annunciation,* from about 1470 (fig. 12); Piermatteo d'Amelia's Gardner image, from about 1480 (fig. 13); or Lorenzo di Credi's interpretation, from the 1490s (fig. 14). The pictorial device can be understood symbolically as an evocation of the infinite mystery of the incarnation, its interposed placement bringing to mind the miraculous crossing between unbridgeable worlds as figured in that moment of Word-turned-flesh. The spatial configuration recalls the Annunciation scene's older, hieratic placement within the church, Gabriel and Mary on arches above and on either side of the altar, where the sacramental mystery unfolds. But such iconographic explication doesn't seem entirely adequate to the peculiarly modern quality of the space these images open up, to the way these scenes seem to manifest in especially pure, which is to say contentless, form the magnetizing properties of the perspective illusion per se. It is hard not to feel a contradiction in the forms of attention they demand, a sense that to yield to their power to captivate is also to be distracted from the momentous scene they reveal. What is the relation between that scene of annunciation—of a female subject being hailed and called into her symbolic destiny—and the way the image itself solicits its beholder, perhaps in its very contradictions announcing and inscribing something momentous there as well?

To approach that question—the question of the interpellating properties of these images as images—first consider the internal logic of the scene. The sense of receiving one's own message back is not restricted to the inverted letters of the address, or to the way that divine "Ave," according to Patristic exegesis, reverses "Eva" and her curse. Take, for instance, Georges Didi-Huberman's observation about the precise symmetry with which the figures of Mary and the Angel are staged on either side of the arch above the altar in the Scrovegni chapel, one scene the reversed image of the other.[3] In less hieratic renderings such as the Annunciations of Van Eyck (fig. 10) or the Master of Flémalle (fig. 15), that mirror symmetry is conveyed in the resemblance between Mary and the angelic messenger. The specular disposition of the figures emphasizes the sense of the event as inward colloquy, even as it heightens the sense of the intercession of the divine word *as* an intercession, a breach, a point evident in those versions of the scene in which God the Father appears in an explicitly triangulated position above and outside the scene, directing His Word between the sacred actors.

Such a disposition conveys in a generalized form the central conceit of the virgin conception—Mary's breached yet intact condition. But

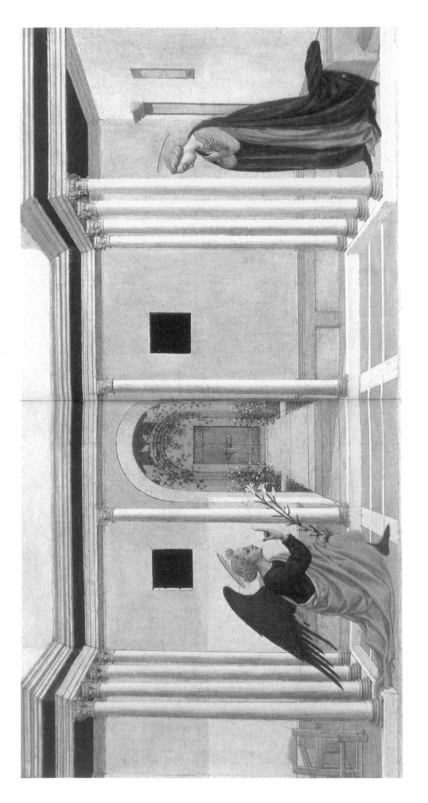

Figure 11. *Annunciation*, by Domenico Veneziano (c.1445).

Reproduced with permission of the Fitzwilliam Museum, Cambridge University, Cambridge, U.K.

Figure 12. *Annunciation,* by Piero della Francesca (c.1470).
Galleria Nazionale dell'Umbria, Perugia, Italy. Reproduced with
permission of Alinari/Art Resource.

Figure 13. *Annunciation,* by Piermatteo d'Amelia (Master of the Gardner
Annunciation) (c.1480). Reproduced with permission of the
Isabella Stewart Gardner Museum, Boston, MA.

Figure 14. *Annunciation*, by Lorenzo di Credi (1597). Uffizi, Florence, Italy.
Reproduced by permission of Alinari/Art Resource.

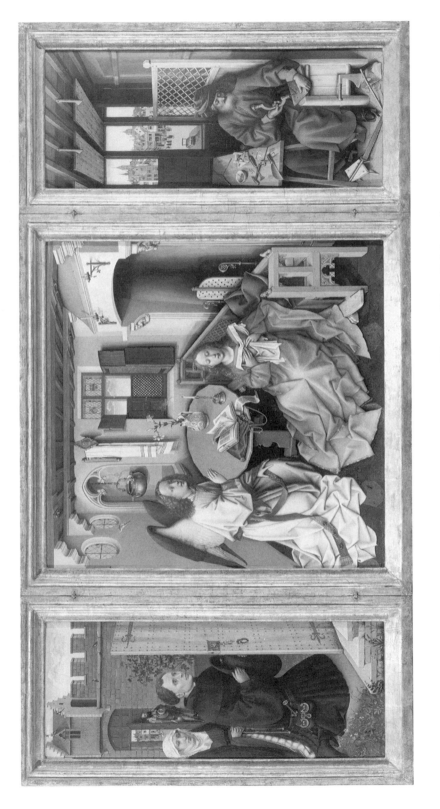

Figure 15. *Mérode Altar*, by Robert Campin (Master of Flémalle) (c.1428).
Reproduced with permission of the Metropolitan Museum of Art, New York, NY.

the mystery of that sacred contradiction is fully recognizable only in terms of how mobile the scene's triangulations in fact are. While the angelic messenger intercedes between God and Mary, God the Father as Logos intercedes between messenger and recipient, an ambiguity suggested by the ease with which God the Father can shift in these representations from an originative position "beyond" the pictorial space—its scene director, as it were (fig. 16)—to a position fully inscribed within the scene as an architectural emblem (fig. 17), as if the mystery of the Logos lies precisely in the equability of those positions within and beyond, of absolute origination and pure mediation. And of course it is Mary herself who traditionally assumes the role of intercessor between the worldly and divine, a function intimated in those representations where Gabriel assumes the posture of devotee directing his gaze to Mary who directs hers above and beyond to God (fig. 18).

That sense that the mystery of the scene is bound up with the circular and illimitable nature of the mediation it describes is given thematic form in the scene's minimal narrative elements. Traditionally, Gabriel is shown interrupting, or about to interrupt, the Virgin at her book of prayers. The scene thus figures symbolic interpellation—the momentous assumption of the divine mandate—as a passage between one instance of textual absorption and the next, as a scene of broken reading. The liminal nature of the moment is literalized in the Metropolitan Museum Annunciation attributed to Petrus Christus, where the Virgin stands at the threshold of the church at the moment her eyes lift from her text to the approaching dove, the stone threshold itself inscribed with her name (fig. 19). Other versions, such as Rogier van der Weyden's, represent the Virgin caught in a moment of meditative distraction between her book and the Angel's call (fig. 20). The transitional nature of the moment signals not so much the simple "fact" of a determinate passage between symbolic dispensations as the mysterious temporality of the address itself, an address that, as Didi-Huberman observes, amounts to a bringing about in the moment of what is still to come and a fulfillment of what had already been prefigured in the sacred text Mary reads.[4]

Inscribed within the narrative scene in the Virgin's role as distracted

75

Figure 16. *Annunciation,* by Piero della Francesca (c.1470). S. Francesco,
Arezzo, Italy. Reproduced with permission of Alinari/Art Resource.

Figure 17. *Annunciation,* by Fra Angelico (c.1434). Museo Diocesano, Cortona, Italy. Reproduced with permission of Alinari/Art Resource.

Figure 18. *Annunciation,* by Ambrogio Lorenzetti (c.1344).
Pinacoteca Nazionale, Siena, Italy. Reproduced with permission
of Alinari/Art Resource.

Figure 19. *Annunciation*, attributed to Petrus Christus (c.1430).
Reproduced with permission of the Metropolitan Museum of Art,
New York, NY.

Figure 20. *Annunciation Triptych* (center panel), by Rogier van der Weyden
(c.1435). Louvre, Paris, France. Reproduced with permission
of Scala/Art Resource.

reader, the play of mediation is also continued without, in the striking way these scenes mark out the viewer's own posture. Consider Fra Angelico's *Annunciation* in the monastery of San Marco, where St. Peter the Martyr appears beyond and to the side of the domed space where the sacred event unfolds (fig. 21). As witness to the scene inscribed in a physical and temporal space beyond it, Peter recalls the triangulating figure of God the Father, even as he functions as image of the worshipful novitiate standing before the painted scene. Such an equation between viewer and God will seem less extravagant understood in terms of the inward, meditative logic of the devotional image, where the worshiper is required to call devoutly to mind the scene that in turn solicits his devotion. The enfolded paradox of our interceding upon a scene of intercession is implied by the Ave Maria the viewer is expressly called upon to repeat before the image, words that mark out the witness as initiator of the scene that solicits him.

Didi-Huberman has subtly analyzed the intricate and sustained way in which these scenes reflect on the mode of their own reception, noting especially the way the central miracle of the *Virginis intacte* is conveyed through the foregrounding of the threshold between viewer and scene, as well as in the inscriptions of opened and closed doorways within the scenes. Filippo Lippi's San Lorenzo *Annunciation* from 1440 is only one of the instances of a frequent illusionistic marking of the threshold of our own witnessing (fig. 22). The empty, delicately invaginated glass vase painted into an illusionistic niche in the foreground threshold of the scene signals the thematic connection between such pictorial effects and the sacred marvel of the penetrated, impenetrable Virgin. "In the Annunciation," Didi-Huberman writes, "there is the conjunction between a distancing and a *virtual crossing* of this same distance by the divine Word or, at another level, by the gift of piety that the devout gaze can show itself capable of."[5] The centrality of the dividing column in images such as this one—"If all Christian knowledge were lost, a person could well suppose that both figures, the Angel Gabriel and Mary, were directing some sort of devout attention to the column that separates them," Michael Baxandall says of another such image—becomes comprehensible insofar as it is taken to figure the "mystery of the threshold" embodied in the

Figure 21. *Annunciation*, by Fra Angelico (1438–50). Convent of San Marco, Cell 3, Florence, Italy. Reproduced with permission of Foto Marburg/Art Resource.

Figure 22. *Annunciation*, by Fra Filippo Lippi (c.1440).
San Lorenzo, Capelli degli Opera, Florence, Italy. Reproduced with
permission of Alinari/Art Resource.

incarnation and thus to figure the sacred in its unfigurability, or in the fact of its limitless figurative displacements.[6] The column "marks both the uncrossable distance and mysterious journey through which the Incarnation has crossed every conceivable threshold. Although it is a 'similitude' by virtue of its verisimilitude to a column in a vaulted edifice, it also becomes a 'dissemblant similitude' where what is most mysterious and most lacking in verisimilitude within Christian faith transits—namely, hypostatic union, the ineffable and 'sublime' union of the human and the divine in a single being."[7]

While Didi-Huberman thus reads the barred space of images such as Filippo Lippi's as entirely continuous with patristic accounts of the mysteries of sacred figuration, it is important to recognize something fundamentally new in the representational economy of such images and in the subjectivity they imply, a break amounting precisely to a breaking away from the thematic content of the scene, sacred or otherwise. Look back for a moment to the Mérode Altarpiece, with its more "archaic" representation of space (fig. 15). The thematic of the *Virginis intacte*, iconographically conveyed in the multiple images of pierced screens—the lattice work across the window, the fireplace screen, the mysterious item Joseph intently works—is also registered in the contradictory space of the representation itself, where the combination of perspective recessions and flattened planes seems at once to draw us in and bring us up short. That contradictory effect is familiar in Northern art during the era and can be attributed either to the primitive stage of the construction of perspective space or to a more coherent effort to retain the iconic, depthless character of the sacred space of the cathedral itself. One might note the contrast between the more naturalistic recession of the two, relatively worldly flanking scenes as against the flattening of the timelessly sacred image in the center, or the way the contradictory—continuous and discontinuous—passageway between the donor's space in the left panel and the central scene mimics the viewer's own relation to the sacred image.

Quattrocento Annunciation images such as the San Lorenzo altar transform that tension into the dimensions of a specular trap, thus converting a property of the object—the very measure of its hieratic closure—into a temporal, "subjectifying" effect. The illusionistic column enacts the temporal ellipsis of the Annunciation in the experience of belatedness and passed boundaries particular to the trompe l'oeil device, the recognition that the truth you seek was right before your eyes all along. The experience of going in deep only to find oneself at the opaque surface of the image—of ending, in a sense, at a point before one began—"embodies" the truth of the breached and inviolate conception. But to the extent that that truth is now conveyed as a performative effect, precisely as a missed encounter with the scene's content, it would be more accurate to see the sacred content as a function of and figure for the image's captivating force. Indeed, the image amounts to a strikingly literal embodiment of the "barred subject," the "$" Lacan posits as the endpoint of the mechanism of interpellation as such, the looping, retroversive passage through the field of symbolization, which consigns the subject to a condition of irreducible belatedness, to emerge always at a point before its entry, without determinable content or ground.[8]

The strongly marked oedipal dimensions of the sacred scene, the fact that it represents symbolic accession in terms of a paternal intervention upon a scene of timeless, vaguely androgynous dyadic rapport, suggests that it wouldn't be wrong to read the "barred Annunciation" as the articulation of an expressly phallic subject. Certainly the exegetes' extravagant, allegorized readings of the column suggest as much. But the "bar" here is phallic just insofar as it can be seen to embody a purely structural effect, its overdetermined "mystery" arising from its capacity to signify the division that founds signification and subject, to function as the one signifier capable of compassing its own founding negation.

The early modern Annunciation is significant in this regard because it reveals the representational logic that sustains that all-important signifying fiction, the fiction that negation "as such," the signifier "as such," might assume a manifest form. To see that, one must recognize how the bar is articulated within the pictorial economy of the picture as a whole, how it emerges at the intersection between two axes in these images, a visual recession in depth, implying or positing a spectatorial subject oriented around its own vanishing and the diegetic scene of hailing. The barring column literalizes the division of attention implied by that double focus. At the same time, that orchestrated chiasmus of sight and language has a grounding force; sight falls subject to language—the bar of symbolic negation—even as that symbolic condition becomes available to specular identification. That suturing concatenation of imaginary and symbolic domains is, I want to argue, the condition for the emergence of a familiarly modern, formal subjectivity, a subject structured upon its capacity to comprehend its own negation and limit. The effect of inwardness thus forged, an inwardness intimating an era still to come, is evident enough in the opaque, knowing gaze of the woman momentarily suspended between absorption and distraction, between reading and seeing (figs. 20, 21).

## 2

The breached, inviolable woman has a life well beyond her devotional incarnations. In the literary/political sphere, she reappears for instance in the figure of the French Princess at the end of Shakespeare's *Henry V* and thus of the Histories, the embodiment of what French law terms the "female bar" and the figure who at once blocks and enables the king's sovereign mastery at the close, in the process structuring an entire political/historical articulation.[9] It is not a coincidence, I would argue, that that elusive constitutive function—the enabling bar—is conjured at the end of the Histories through a perspective trope brought to bear on a woman:

> King Henry: You may . . . thank love for my blindness, who
> cannot see many a fair French city for one fair
> French maid that stands in my way.
> French King: Yes, my Lord, you see them perspectively: the
> cities turn'd into a maid; for they are all girdled
> with maiden walls that war has never ent'red.
>                                                 (5.2.316–23)

But to explore in a more nuanced way the pertinence of these Annunciation images to the symbolic articulation of the modern political and historical subject, I'd like to turn to a different Shakespearean context, a scene within a play concerned with the fate of the subject in a profoundly desacralized world. In the famous "Dover Cliffs" scene in *King Lear,* instead of the visual representation of a moment of verbal solicitation, one is presented with a literary representation of a perspective effect, Edgar's remarkable illusionistic evocation of the (imaginary) view downward.[10] And, instead of an Annunciation, one has what amounts to an exorcism. Disguised as a Bedlam beggar, Edgar leads his blind and despairing father to what Gloucester takes to be the cliffs of Dover. Edgar describes the view:

> Come on, sir; here's the place: stand still. How fearful
> And dizzy 'tis to cast one's eyes so low!
> The crows and choughs that wing the midway air
> Show scarce so gross as beetles; half way down
> Hangs one that gathers sampire, dreadful trade!
> Methinks he seems no bigger than his head.
> The fishermen that walk upon the beach
> Appear like mice, and yond tall anchoring bark
> Diminish'd to her cock, her cock a buoy
> Almost too small for sight. The murmuring surge,
> That on th'unnumber'd idle pebble chafes,
> Cannot be heard so high. I'll look no more,
> Lest my brain turn, and deficient sight
> Topple down headlong. (4.6.11–24)[11]

The force of the description isn't entirely evident, I think, until the equivocal theatrical moment that follows it, the moment where Gloucester, kneeling, "throws himself forward and falls," hitting the stage, unconscious. What keeps Gloucester's "fall" from being a queasy theatrical joke at the expense of the blind, pathos-ridden old man? Without ruling out the fathomless reserves of self-protective sadism this play is capable of mobilizing, one might understand the effect by extending one's sense of who the joke is on. Even if one doesn't believe that Edgar has actually led us to the cliffs of Dover—there are sufficient clues that he is engaged in a deception—and even if at some level one doesn't ever entirely forget one is in a theater, the moment where Gloucester topples two feet and hits the floor comes as a jolt after

Edgar's evocation of the vertiginous view down. The scene amounts to the equivalent of the moment where Wile E. Coyote, who certainly should know better by now, runs full tilt into the mountain on which his more wily adversary has painted a recession to infinity. Or, to be truer to its odd tonalities, the scene is the equivalent of the moment we bump up against the column at the dead center of the Annunciation.

Such moments of self-forgetfulness are not incidental to the play: Consider the Fool's maddening, curative power to distract the King from himself, for instance, or the extraordinary exchange between Kent and Albany late in the play. We have just seen the duel between Edmund and Edgar, heard Edgar's account of his last moments with his father, and heard of the deaths of Goneril and Regan, when Kent arrives:

> Kent:                                    I am come
>      To bid my King and master aye good night;
>      Is he not here?
> Albany:                         Great thing of us forgot!
>      Speak, Edmund, where's the King? And where's
>      Cordelia?
>      Seest thou this object, Kent?
>      [*The bodies of Goneril and Regan are brought in.*]
> (5.3.233–37)

The accusation of forgetfulness bears most pointedly on the audience, of course, for it was aware that Edmund had earlier sent the writ against the lives of Lear and Cordelia. No "object" has concerned the spectators more in the tragedy than that dire end. What does it mean that one could have fatally lost track of Lear and Cordelia? If one is momentarily caught up in "trifles"—"That's but a trifle here," says Albany at the news of Edmund's death moments later—that can either be a testament to the distracting powers of display or a more guilty sign of a desire for such distraction. On the other hand, it would be as true to say that it is one's desire to keep the "object" firmly in view that distracts; it is precisely their blazoned promise of explanatory closure that gives absorptive power to the final duel and Edgar's fatally punctuating tale of his father's end, where death concides precisely, killingly, with narrative closure. To the extent that the bind feels unresolvable, to the extent that the fixed and the averted gaze alike betray, the tragedy might seem to be about the irreducibility of distraction, with the "object" it brings to view being nothing other than the audience's own saving, disastrous forgetfulness.

Like the scenes of Annunciation, the cliff scene gives dramatic form to that absorption and self-forgetfulness—the subject as barred subject. But it also suggests what there is of the subject beyond that being oriented around its own limit-point. To see that beyond, one needs to view the scene from another angle: from below. After Gloucester rouses from his faint, Edgar, still disguised but now shifted into the part of a Cornwall peasant, describes the old man's miraculous fall:

| | |
|---|---|
| Edgar: | This is above all strangeness. |
| | Upon the crown o'th'cliff what was that |
| | Which parted from you? |
| Gloucester: | A poor unfortunate beggar. |
| Edgar: | As I stood here below methought his eyes |
| | Were two full moons; he had a thousand noses, |
| | Horns whelk'd and wav'd like the enridged sea: |
| | It was some fiend: therefore, thou happy father, |
| | Think that the clearest Gods, who make them honours |
| | Of men's impossibilities, have preserved thee. |
| Gloucester: | I do remember now; henceforth I'll bear |
| | Affliction till it do cry out itself |
| | 'Enough, enough,' and die. That thing you speak of |
| | I took it for a man; often 'twould say |
| | 'The Fiend, the Fiend': he led me to that place. |

$$(4.6.66-79)$$

The son thus stages his father's "fall" as an instance of divine intercession and as revelation of a new symbolic destiny, or, more grimly, the revival of an old and blind commitment to endure. "Interpellation" in this case would thus seem to be largely a matter of calculated therapeutic management. Indeed, it wouldn't be hard to detect a measure of infantilization in Edgar's fantastical description of the fiend, an aggressive "trifling" with the gullible father who was so easily turned against him. "Why I do trifle with his despair is done to cure him," he says in an oddly explanatory aside. Edgar himself raises the ethical question of his continued disguise toward the end; "and never (O fault) revealed myself until this moment" he says at the point where he is finally "armed" to assume his identity again (5.3.91,92). But the question is evident from the outset if we accept that he overhears his father's words when he first comes upon him after his blinding: "Oh! Dear son Edgar, / The food of thy abused father's wrath; / Might I but live to see thee in my touch, / I'd say I had eyes again" (4.1.21–24). To refuse that blind call is to refuse much.

Then again, the cliff scene is noteworthy precisely because it coincides with the moment at which Edgar is no longer able to sustain his disguise and distance. As they approach the cliff:

| | |
|---|---|
| Gloucester: | Methinks thy voice is alter'd, and thou speak'st |
| | In better phrase and matter than thou didst. |
| Edgar: | You're much deceiv'd; in nothing am I chang'd |
| | But in my garments. |
| Gloucester: | Methinks you're better spoken. (4.6.7–10) |

To recognize that Edgar betrays himself in the scene is to recognize the self-referential dimension of his description of the "Fiend" that had led his father to the cliff's edge, to recognize how deeply Edgar, too, had been playing out the fantasy of his father's death, testing his own demonic, and thoroughly oedipal, inclinations. The strangely speculative and slightly defensive commentary the son enters into over his father's momentarily unconscious body suggests as much:

> Gone, sir: farewell,
> And yet I know not how conceit may rob
> The treasury of life when life itself
> Yields to the theft; had he been where he thought
> By this had thought been past. Alive or dead?
> Ho, you sir! friend! Hear you, sir! speak!
> Thus might he pass indeed; yet he revives. (4.6.41–47)

The scene should be read as an exorcism of the figure that orchestrates it, then, as much as of the one he "redeems."

In other words, one should not assume that Edgar is in a position of mastery in relation to the scene of transformation, or that the view from below is merely a naïve pendant to the powerfully seductive view from above. Within the purely fictitious space of the play, why does one credit the view down rather than the view up? Gloucester's susceptibility to the illusionistic description is specifically bound up with his susceptibility to the temptation of the eye. Whereas the penalty for the king who loses himself to the signs he himself orchestrates is madness, the penalty for the suspicious man, the man who defines his powers over and against the concealing signifiers of the world, is blindness. The scene of Gloucester's blinding—the horrific extrusion of his eyes—is picked up in the description of the threat posed by the vertiginous view:

> How fearful
> . . . . . 'tis to cast one's eyes so low!
> . . . . . . . . I'll look no more,
> Lest my brain turn, and the deficient sight
> Topple down headlong. (4.6.11–24) [12]

To account for the scene's power to "topple" sight, it is necessary to recognize what makes Edgar's description historically and philosophically striking, that is, that the passage can be read both as an evocation of rationalized, perspectivally ordered Cartesian or Albertian space and as a harbinger of the Kantian sublime, with its passage to the limit, the point where apprehension exceeds itself and "the brain turns." Those symbolic/philosophical systems converge in the passage around the trope that underwrites both. The illusionistic "reality effect" is a function of the combination of rhetorical self-reference—of closure—and illimitability particular to metonymy: the "sampire gatherer" diminished to his own "head," the "bark" to its "cock" or dinghy, the cock to its "buoy": the conversion of whole to part sustains a purely self-referential and self-sustaining signifying chain on the condition of that chain's indefinite extension.

The passage suggests the rhetorical basis of perspective, understood

as a system of proportional ratios oriented around limitless extension.[13] It may also suggest how bound up that indefinitely substi-
tutive structure is with a specifically economic conception: note the
reference to the sampire gatherer's "dreadful trade" (15). More significant, though, is the implied relation between such a rhetorical
structure and the subjectivity it implies. For it is precisely that closed,
self-referential economy that subjects the subject to the unchecked
sliding of the metonymic chain. The rhetoric of contiguity specific
to the empirical effect—and thus historically constitutive of the subject as subject of vision, as Cartesian subject—simultaneously subjects
that masterful being to its own annulment, a threat that assumes a
specifically visual form. Indeed, in properly Kantian fashion, such a
passage to the limit can be understood as the condition for that subject's supersensory mastery. Whether the threat posed by the passage
is real, as Edgar momentarily imagines it to have been for his father,
or imaginary, as one comes to realize it may have been for Edgar, is
ultimately less significant than the way the passage stages the very
movement into figurativeness as a function of the limit. To speak of
the "murmuring surge / That . . . / Cannot be heard so high" is to
relocate figuration not as the condition for empirical apprehension
but in the determinate, if retroactively realized, passage beyond such
apprehension.

To puncture the heady effect of the passage, as Gloucester does
when he hits the stage, is not simply to undo perspectival illusion-
ism in the name of the empirical "reality" of the stage; it is, in a more
thoroughgoing way, to subvert the entire mechanism of empiricist ap-
perception and the subjectivity implied by it. What opens beyond that
reality effect is not the material-real, but another space altogether:

> As I stood here below methought his eyes
> Were two full moons; he had a thousand noses,
> Horns whelk'd and wav'd like the enridged sea:
> It was some fiend. (4.6.69–72)

Edgar's self-exorcizing description answers to the fatal view from
above precisely in the flagrancy of its theatricality. If in perspectiv-
ism it is the subject's constitution in relation to a determinate ob-

ject world, precisely as what is not in the "picture," that subjects it to the scene's undertow, here the subject is conjured from the outset as something at once inward and alien, haunting demon and pure artifice. There is loss here, too, but rather than being focalized in the threatening, galvanizing illusion of infinitude, it is now played out in a dispersal that fabulously mingles subject and scene: a thousand noses, eyes like moons, horns like "the enridged sea" viewed a moment ago from afar. The point is not simply that the subject is now seen from without, as object of the gaze. In a more radical sense the description inverts seeing, as if one viewed one's self from the other end of the perspective cone. With the eyes as "two full moons," the atavistic, all-seeing eye implicit in the scene before becomes indistinguishable from the splayed and empty eye of spectacle. Again, this recalls Lacan's claim that the "underside" of Cartesian consciousness — a consciousness founded on the illusion of the self "seeing itself see itself" and thus overseeing its own vanishing — makes itself felt in the more uncanny, reverting, "inside-out structure of the gaze."[14] In the place of the "brain turn[ing]" and sight "toppl[ing]" at the limit-point of empirical subjectivity, then, is an archaic being, "whelk'd and wav'd" through and through. Kenneth Muir hears in the line an echo of Golding's *Metamorphoses:* "Joves ymage which the Lybian folke by name of Hammon serve, / Is made with crooked welked hornes that in ward still do terve."[15]

Does this image, clearly a figure for the theatrical spectator's own absorbed, dispersed gaze, suggest a space beyond the phallic bar and the subject constituted as pure negation? The scene of exorcism is, of course, as oedipally determined as are the scenes of Annunciation. With its absurdly multiplied noses, with its "horns" — always the joking, manly/unmanned image of the cuckold — the scene is phallic indeed. But the very multiplicity of its apotropisms, a fixitiveness that enacts its own dispersal, the fact that the phallus "itself" in this case amounts to a curious form of ossified wavering (a horn "like the enridged sea") suggests at least a different staging of desire, one, indeed, in which desire is explicitly an effect of the staging or framing that brings it to view.

In other words, what opens beyond the perspectival subject is the subject as subject of fantasy, understanding fantasy not as the conjuring of an imaginary object of desire but as the frame that supplies the very coordinates of desire and thus the space within which the subject is suspended and multiply inscribed.[16] Fantasy sustains the subject not in relation to a determinate object or limit but in the very movement—the "inward terv[ing]"—through which it at once conjures and eludes itself in fantasy.[17] Historically, what may be most immediately striking about such a fantasy space is the way its hieratic image—an expressly idolatrous image, judging from Golding—seems to hearken not just beyond but also before the perspectival subject, perhaps even evoking in demonized form the experience of divine "ecstasis," of standing outside oneself, implied by the splayed or inverted perspective construction of the premodern iconic image.[18]

3

Edgar's theatrical fantasy would seem to suggest a passage beyond the perspectival subject articulated in the scenes of Annunciation. Does it imply the representational limits of the early modern subject? To answer that, one must consider the play's larger engagements with the question of interpellation, especially in relation to sexuality. *King Lear* begins, in fact, with a scene of barred interpellation: Cordelia's refusal to speak the words demanded of her, the famous "nothing, my lord" that precipitates the tragedy. She is responding, of course, to a demand for a freely offered proof of love from a father, not to a narrative destiny imposed by God. "What can you say to draw / A third more opulent than your sisters? Speak" (1.1.84–85). But to understand the often-remarked starkness of Cordelia's refusal, one must see the opening exchange as the inscribing mandate it is.

Lear's daughters are called on to speak the words that will win for them the lots that have already been ordained them; we know that two of the three portions of land have been apportioned, and for Lear, the entire ritual test transpires at the level of the sign and in something approaching a future anterior tense: "Which of you shall we say doth love us most?" (1.2.50). And yet, the transparent theatricality of the test—the fact that it is so obviously "merely" symbolic—doesn't make it any less absolute. The ritual exchange is disquieting precisely because it is so annihilatingly complete. In exchange for Goneril and Regan yielding up sensate life ("I love you more than word can wield the matter / Dearer than eye-sight, space and liberty"; "I profess / Myself an enemy to all other joys / Which the most precious square of sense possesses"), Lear reconstitutes phenomenal life and space from their sparest signifiers:

> Of all these bounds, even from this line to this,
> With shadowy forests and with champains rich'd,
> With plenteous rivers and wide-skirted meads,
> We make thee lady. (1.1.62–65)

This is, of course, a performance, but one that is not so easily penetrated. Recognizing the overt staginess of Lear's ritual, critics have taken his response to Cordelia's refusal as narcissistic rage at the undoing of his preordained performance. And yet, Lear is never more theatrical nor more rhetorically ornate and controlled than he is when he turns on his daughter:

> For, by the sacred radiance of the sun,
> The mysteries of Hecate and the night,
> By all the operation of the orbs
> From whom we do exist and cease to be,
> Here I disclaim all my paternal care,
> Propinquity and property of blood,
> And as a stranger to my heart and me
> Hold thee from this forever. The barbarous Scythian,
> Or he that makes his generation messes
> To gorge his appetite, shall to my bosom
> Be as well neighbour'd, pitied, and reliev'd,
> As thou my sometime daughter. (1.1.108–19)

Is Lear beyond the performance here, even beyond premeditation? Remember that Lear has orchestrated the occasion to give his youngest in marriage, as well as to partition the kingdom; the very abruptness of his judgment against Cordelia might suggest a self-protective will to banish the beloved child who is about to leave him. At the same time, Lear's banishment assures that Cordelia is matched with the husband who loves her, a match Lear makes a point of overseeing even after he has repudiated her. Can repudiation be an act of love? Lear's oddly self-revealing invocation of the "barbarous Scythian" "that makes his generation his messes" suggests a premonitory awareness about his incestuous inability to distinguish himself from the objects of his love.[19] In relation to that obscure knowledge, banishment might indeed become hard to distinguish from protectiveness, as if Lear were violently placing her beyond his own violent ken, beyond the rapidly dissolving frame of the play itself.

This is, of course, to find in Lear's "darker purpose" motives dark to himself, to see him as at once the most impossibly obtuse and impossibly knowing character in the play. In fact, one can feel, especially in the dreamlike indirections of his final "recognition" scene with Cordelia, that the tragedy has entailed Lear's coming to know what he in some sense has known all along. But the overdetermination of the King's actions at the opening should be read not in terms of depth psychology but as an effect of a mechanism of symbolization that goes beyond any of the play's agents, as it does the limits of the play itself. The severity of Cordelia's refusal to accede to her part in the exchange is sign enough of her awareness of the omnivorous and annihilating nature of the symbolic exchange to which she is being called. And yet the stark "nothing" that refuses the terms of the mandate is at some level indistinguishable from the negation that founds and renews that inscribing mechanism, that interpellates one in one's proper place within the unfolding drama.

The play's well-known preoccupation with the meaning of "nothing" is bound up with the irreducibility of that double bind, the entrapments of interpellation as such. Whereas Lear falls because he imagines "nothing can come of nothing," that is, from a literality that fails to conceive a beyond to his signifying universe, Gloucester falters precisely because he imagines there must be such a beyond. "The quality of nothing hath not such need to hide itself. . . . Let's see: come; if it be nothing, I shall not need spectacles" (1.2.33–35), he says, falling easily for Edmund's staged concealment of the letter he's forged to falsely incriminate his brother. To define oneself against the absorptively self-referential king, to stake one's mastery on the assumption that one knows theater for the empty thing it is, is to inscribe oneself as a Gloucester, all the more blind for imagining one can see the performance for what it is.

A preoccupation with the illimitability of the symbolic domain is hardly unique to *King Lear;* one might think of the ways in which the choral epilogues in Shakespeare's comedies play upon the audience's anxious and inevitably self-ensnaring desire to know where the fiction ends. In some sense, the prominence of such an effect in *King Lear*—the way the play stages the question of its own limits as a thematic preoccupation from the outset—is of a piece with the play's concern with sovereignty and its symbolic function. Indeed, the scandalous conceit the King plays out at the outset, the fantasy that one might in a sense oversee one's own demise, merely gives dramatic form to an extravagancy implicit in the concept of sovereignty. According to late Medieval political/theological doctrine, the king's body was a double body, his true, corporate/symbolic body existing over and beyond the mortal one and most visible at its death. Insofar as it is constituted by that symbolic supplement—insofar as that is its essence—sovereignty can be seen to originate in the passage beyond its own limit, a passage that thus amounts at once to the purest measure of regal omnipotence and to a manifestation of the obscure workings of the death drive; among other things, it is Lear's intended "crawl toward death" that is thwarted at the outset (1.1.40).

Still, the outright and vertiginous nature of *King Lear*'s opening gesture of inscribing its symbolic mandate or condition within itself suggests that the fiction of the sovereign's body is subject to a larger social/symbolic transformation. Claude Lefort describes the shift from a premodern order in which the social body is grounded in an external transcendent source to a distinctly modern one in which the social seeks its ground solely from within itself, a necessary and impossible recourse that constitutes the social dimension precisely as a social dimension, as an irreducibly contingent and untotalizable space.[20] Cordelia's "nothing"—the "female bar" that sets the play in motion—gives gendered form to that elliptical foundation. In a sense, it precipitates the passage from ritual into history, from the pure circuit of sovereign demand to tragic contingency. But it does so through a gesture that, inscribed within the transformation it brings about, marks the symbolic space it opens as a space without determinable advent or horizon.

And yet, for all its apparent inescapability, the ritual staging of symbolic interpellation at the opening is not the only version the play offers. Lear's well-known instance of male hysteria recalls the scene of exorcism: "O! How this mother swells up toward my heart; / *Hysterica passio!* Down, thou climbing sorrow," Lear exclaims. Noting the variant spelling of the Latin term in the early folios, Richard Halpern suggests the relation between that hysterical state, known as "the suffocation of the mother," and the fact of social and historical inscription:

> "*Historica passio*" [is] the bearing or enduring or manifestation of historical force through one's person and one's body. . . . What Lear feels rising up within him, overcoming him, is that conversion hysteria which constitutes him as a dramatic character and invests his every gesture with a richness of historical signification. Lear experiences his dramatic birth in a particularly traumatic way, whose intensity illuminates the process more generally, just as dramatic representation itself offers a dense and revealing image of our own constitution as social agents.[21]

Halpern's historicizing account is an implicit rejoinder to those more or less ahistorical feminist psychoanalytic analyses that treat the "suffocating mother" in relation to the threat posed to masculine self-identity by the figure who has been notably excluded from the symbolic universe of the play.[22] But the textual slippage Halpern notes suggests a compelling point of intersection between such psychoanalytic readings, with all they bring to bear concerning gender and sexuality, and subject formation conceived as a historical "event." To attend to that complex space of interpellation in a way that is neither universalizing nor crudely deterministic may mean attending to the fact of rhetorical slippage itself, the ambiguity that in this instance both opens and suspends the relation between the psychoanalytic and the historical.

To understand the connection between hysterica—or historica—passio and symbolic inscription as such, one must turn to the point in the play when the condition returns: Lear's riveting final address.

> Lear:    And my poor fool is hang'd! No, no, no life!
> Why should a dog, a horse, a rat, have life,
> And thou no breath at all? Thou'lt come no more,
> Never, never, never, never, never!
> Pray you, undo this button: thank you, Sir.
> Do you see this? Look on her, look, her lips,
> Look there, look there!   [Dies.]
>
> Edgar:    He faints! My Lord, my Lord.
> Kent:    Break, heart; I prithee, break!
> Edgar:    Look up, my Lord. (5.3.304–13)

This is the moment in the play when something comes of nothing; Lear's hanging upon Cordelia's silent lips hearkens back to her "Nothing, my Lord," the thwarting rejoinder that precipitates the tragedy and Lear's reply: "Nothing will come of nothing: speak again." Nor is one in a position to say that Lear is merely in a state of delusion when he calls on us at the end to look there. The apparently mutually exclusive and equally blinding alternative in the play between seeing nothing as nothing or taking it as a mask for something, between reading literally or figuratively, dissolves at the point where the boundary between living and dead wavers—where Lear himself yields—and death as ultimate guarantor of the distinction between fictitious and real, literal and figurative, begins to falter. The long awaited "recognition" occurs, not in the play, but where the play exceeds one's ability to compass its limits and thus to constitute oneself in relation to its boundary, to know whether one is placed inside or outside its field.

What does it mean that this moment where the play goes beyond itself, where it becomes truly performative, should also be the moment when the "mother" returns? "Pray you, undo this button." Muir glosses the line: "Lear feels a sense of suffocation, and imagines it is caused by the tightness of his clothes."[23] The return of the mother here should be understood, I think, in relation to what is most striking formally about these last moments: not that "nothing" returns—not that negation "as such" comes to the fore—but that it returns in such a vividly specular form.

> I know when one is dead, and when one lives;
> She's dead as earth. Lend me a looking-glass;
> If that her breath will mist or stain the stone,
> Why, then she lives. (5.3.259–62)

We are reminded of the Fool's reference to women making "mouths in a glass" (3.2.35), as well as Edmund's reference to Goneril's "speaking looks." At the end, the implied convergence of speech and sight intensifies to an invocation of the onlookers within and beyond the play: "Look on her, look, her lips, / Look there, look there!"

Given the misogynistic anxieties the play persistently mobilizes, as well as the familiar equation of lips and female genitals ("down . . . your element is below"), such a moment could be read as an explicitly hysterical instance of the masculine claim to the visible, empirically demonstrable nature of feminine lack: to *see* nothing, and to see it *there*. But here, specular identification is bound up with a far more unstable form of transference, one which can be felt as a disturbance in language's referential capacity to determine where, precisely, the disturbance is arising. "Pray you, undo this button": whose button, annotators have asked, Cordelia's or his own? Is this a case of hysterical identification with the strangled child or hysterical projection onto her? Is this the act that frees breath or causes the suffocating Mother to rise? Such equivocations occur because of the foundational character of the transference involved, a specular identification not with any object but with the "nothing" constitutive of sign and subject alike, a moment Julia Kristeva describes as "the hallucination of nothing."[24] However minimal it may seem, the interpretive force implied by that arbitrary positing—the force required to button matters down, not in the name of a determinate content but to establish a relation to symbolization as such—carries a massive charge in the play, associated as it is with the suffocating "act" that constitutes the tragedy. The fact that that act is metaphorically and transferentially identified with the mother is indication enough that it is that not merely barred but exorcized figure who is the arbitrary locus of such founding violence and is thus the figure whose sacrifice enables the symbolic function to assume its apparently neutral and supervenient form.

Lear's final injunction—"Look, her lips / Look there"—brings us back to the intersection of sight and language in the scene of Annunciation, the crossing that made that scene a scene of interpellation. Far from securing symbolic negation in manifest form, Lear's words suggest precisely how aleatory and forced that relation is. The chiasmus of imaginary and symbolic registers in the Annunciation "manages" a fundamental contradiction, one that enabled the founding fiction of the sign capable of signifying its own negation: the notion that difference, the bar of signification, can be understood at once as what breaches specular identification and as the object *of* such identification. Lear's "Look there" exposes that aporia between identification and difference in its own posited condition; the tightening reflexive gyre between Lear and Cordelia, between living and dead, between speech and lips, reaches its signifying limit in a deixis that, pointing to nothing beyond itself, remains suspended between self-signifying sign and mute, inscribing mark. As much as the Annunciation—the Mother inscribed—articulates the paradigmatic condition for interpellation as a formal mechanism, "Hysteria passio"—the possessing mother—gives name to that point where such a mechanism inevitably exceeds itself, that is, where it fails.

Returning to the Dover cliffs, one can now recognize that scene's historical and ideological significance. Lear's final "Look there" recalls the cliff scene insofar as both are a matter of being enjoined to see what isn't there. But while the earlier account both seduces and "undoes" sight, proves it to be subject to the limitless ensnarements of a purely symbolic function, the final moments of the play suggest that a certain form of specular cathexis nevertheless remains as the very ground, or the groundless ground, of symbolization. Whatever it suggests of discontinuity and dispersal, the scene of fantasy ultimately functions as a support of symbolization understood as an autonomous function: through that thematized exorcism, symbolization stages its demonic beyond in figurable form, shoring against the far more unstable foreclosure that underwrites the very terms of the drama of subjective loss, the structuring oppositions between metonymy and metaphor, between empirical space and fantasy, between negation and its iconic beyond.[25]

To recognize the historical and political character of that articulation, one needs to recall what is distinctive about the role of the character it concerns. Edgar will go on to assume the mantle of power from his elders at the close, a transition whose generational nature the play strongly marks. Although he assumes his power only after he ritually reclaims his name, the ostentation of that carefully staged scene merely reinforces one's sense that Edgar's distinction hinges less on lineal claims than on his proven capacities as a self-inventing subject, a new kind of autochthonous, "self-fashioning" person.[26] How does one reconcile Edgar's "possession" with his status as man of his own making? In fact, the two conditions are entirely of a piece. To see that, one must consider the relation between fantasy and the political formation with whose emergence the abstract, autonomous subject is bound up. With the advent of the modern state, Jacqueline Rose writes,

> something irrational—not as in unreasonable, but as in relying on a power no reason can account for—has entered the polity. . . . Once real authority is no longer invested in the prince and his trappings, it loses its face and disembodies itself: "With this analysis of the state as an omnipotent yet impersonal power," Quentin Skinner concludes his study of the foundations of modern political thought, "we may be said to enter the modern world." The modern state enacts its authority as ghostly, fantasmatic authority. But it would be wrong to deduce from this—like those who misread Freud's attention to fantasy as essentially trivializing—that the state is any the less real for that.[27]

The association between the moment where "authority loses its face and disembodies itself"—the moment Skinner associates with the passage into the "modern world"—and *King Lear*'s thematic preoccupations is clear enough. More suggestive is the connection between that transformation—the emergence of the state understood as at once constitutive and spectral, a formation that supersedes any of the subjects who make it up—and the appearance of a phantasmatic subject. Edgar's abjectness in the play, the mysterious guilt of the good son evident in his abrupt assumption of a role whose squalor and madness goes well beyond its function as disguise, should be understood as a function not of personal history but of this emerging and over-determined relation to the domain of state and law. "It should . . . come as no surprise," Rose goes on to remark, "to notice the curious but striking proximity between this account of modern statehood and the superego, that part of the mind which Freud eventually theorized as the site of social law. For Freud, the superego exerts an authority beyond all reason, implacable to the precise extent that it draws on all the unconscious energies it is meant to tame. . . . Which is why inside the head, the law always feels a bit crazy and why, although it never stops trying, it can never quite justify itself. Like the state, the superego is both ferocious and a bit of a fraud."[28]

Despite all its apparent archaism, then, demonic possession amounts, precisely in its mixture of outright staginess and intractability, to the subjective index and counterpart to the emergence of the abstract categories of state and law. The political character of the cliff scene's strangely composite and theatrical demon becomes discernable, perhaps, if seen to anticipate the multiform figure that looms up over the horizon of the frontispiece to *Leviathan,* Hobbes's political treatise that belatedly attempts to reclaim for the king's body a power more phantasmatic and apparitional than it ever had.[29]

The splitting off of fantasy, its emergence as the necessary demonic beyond of the perspectival subject, can thus be taken as an index of the appearance of the modern political subject, the subject possessed amounting to the other face of the modern possessive individual. But one should consider what that association between modernity and fantasy means for the project of historicizing subjectivity. The temporalization of the subject implied by the barred annunciation is of a piece with the construction of the fiction of continuous recession, of horizons and vanishing points in these images, a fiction that in turn underwrites any historicist account. The cliff scene shows the modern subject, that expressly temporal/historical being, to be inseparable from the break through which it simultaneously becomes groundless and phantasmatic. To the extent that the psychoanalytic subject is always a subject in and of fantasy, it would not be wrong to say that the psychoanalytic subject and the subject of historicism amount to the reverse "inward terv[ing]" face of one another. Does the abyssal, reflexively undecidable relation between history and theory thus implied merely reinscribe the question of the subject within its own endless recession? The unspoken exorcism that marks the conclusion of the play—the one for and against which the visible drama of demonic exorcism stands—implies the absolute contingency and blind force that underwrite any such explanatory recourse to pure, resolving infinitude.

# Chapter 4

# Dumb Hamlet

My Dear Greg,

You will not agree with this book; I am not at all sure you will like it; but it is yours, whether you like it or not. And I dedicate it to you, without asking your permission, as a trifling retaliation for the spell you put upon me (without asking my permission) eighteen years ago, a spell which changed the whole tenor of my existence, and still dominates it in part. You may have guessed something of this, but you cannot know it all; and as the story of how you forced yourself into my life will explain to others the origin and purpose of this book, you must bear with the telling of it. —J. Dover Wilson, *What Happens in* Hamlet

The story that Wilson proceeds to tell in this 1935 dedicatory epistle amounts to one of the more hyperbolic episodes in the annals of interpretive crisis.[1] Traveling on a train in 1917 and distracting himself from the weightier matters of that weighty time, Wilson opened the then current issue of *The Modern Language Review* and happened on an article by the critic, W. W. Greg. "But this was no ordinary number, for it opened with an article by you that might have thrown any mind off its balance, an article ominously entitled 'Hamlet's Hallucination.'" What was the argument that "changed the whole tenor" of one man's "existence" and amounted to "a turning-point in the history of Shakespearian criticism"? Claudius, Greg observes, does not react to the pantomime that serves as a prologue to the play within the play, the dumb show that exposes the crime directly before his eyes. Therefore, Greg concludes, Claudius must be innocent, the Ghost's account of the crime false, and the ghost himself a hallucination.

As Terence Hawkes has argued, Wilson's crisis can be associated with anxieties over the political upheavals of the critic's own day: labor unrest at home, revolution abroad.[2] But such direct reference to dire context fails to engage what is most striking about the scene, what makes Wilson's reponse (only the most personalized of the barrage of retorts Greg's "discovery" prompted from more than a decade of Shakespeareans) so odd and so exemplary as an instance of interpretive crisis. For what prompts outrage in this case, what threatens to unhinge many a temperate critical mind, is, quite simply, Claudius's peculiar lack of outrage at the dumb show's outrageous imputation.

Why doesn't Claudius respond? More precisely, why doesn't he respond to the prologue, which mimics precisely the details of the crime, whereas he *does* respond to the play-within-the-play proper, which represents the crime in more veiled form? Greg's article prompted a flood of explanations: Claudius doesn't react because he's not paying attention; he doesn't react because the effect is cumulative; the problem is exaggerated because Claudius's response, when it comes, is more muted than critics imagine; the problem doesn't actually exist because Shakespeare wasn't concerned with details of plot anyway.[3] The only option critics have not proposed is that Claudius does not respond because he is absorbed.

What strains credibility in such a reading is not the idea that one could get lost in a play but that Claudius could forget himself before *this* scene. And yet the truth directly revealed can have such an effect. "I have words to speak in thine ear will make thee dumb," Hamlet proclaims on his return from England (4.6.24–25).[4] The dumb show suggests why this should be the case. For what is the truth the scene conveys, the ear-poisoning crime, but the image of Claudius's, and of course our own, theatrical captivation? The primal transgression we search out at the dark center of the drama remains elusive only because it is too close to view, consisting as it does in our own attention.[5]

Claudius fails to react to the dumb show not because he misses the deed but because, in a sense, he *can't* miss it; it inheres in his response. His outrage, when it comes, is that his outrage alone betrays him, an empty, inescapable, and hystericizing effect that precipitates flight. The "mousetrap" appears to entrap absolutely, for it is not merely a remediable instance of absorption but Claudius's own response to his captivation that captures him. It is such a performative, boundary-dissolving effect that moves like "false fire" (3.2.266) from the text to the field of critical response.[6] Claudius's belatedness and captivation presage that which lends Wilson's response the force of spell and trauma: the sense that something has slipped past one's guard, that boundaries have dissolved, that the mind has turned on itself.

The effect is not confined to kings and attentive men of letters. The dumb show suggests much about theater's well-known capacity to provoke outrage of a notably virulent and ostentatious order. During Shakespeare's era, the theater was endlessly likened to a "contagion" and an "infectious sight," even seen as the source of plague, because the threat it posed remained troublingly indistinguishable from the response it provoked.[7] That fact made theater more threatening than any real transgression. "Onlie the filthiness of plaies, and spectacles is such as maketh both actors and beholders guiltie alike," Anthony Munday wrote.[8] Simply to articulate the problem risks renewing it: "For som sinnes, though most hainous, may wel and honestlie both be named, and blamed too, as murder theft, adulterie, sacriledge, and such like; onlie the filthiness of theaters are such as may not honestlie be not so much as blamed."[9] Against such a danger, we have no choice but to "shut up our orifices," Stephen Gosson declares, as if with an anxious eye and ear trained on the scene of ear poisoning.[10]

In its bracing emptiness, the scene of outrage reveals something about the precise mechanics of power in *Hamlet*, as well as in the profoundly stagy culture from which the play derives. Against a Foucauldian reading of the play based on claims for a disciplinary regime of spectacularly unmediated authority, the dumb show suggests that the paranoiac apprehension about unseen seers that energizes the drama from beginning to end conceals the more riveting prospect that the gaze behind the arras, the gaze that endlessly steals the sovereign subject from himself, is his own. The play's darkest secrets always entail, at their most irreducible, just such impossible visibility.

But that I am forbid

.  .  .  .  .  .  .  .  .  .  .  .  .

I could unfold a tale whose lightest word
Would  .  .  .  .  .  .  .  .  .  .  .
Make thy two eyes like stars start from their spheres,
Thy knotted and combined locks to part,
And each particular hair to stand on end,
Like quills upon the fearful porpentine. (1.5.13–20)

The combination of fragmentation—extruded eyes—and medusa-like fixity in the Ghost's account makes sense when one realizes that what holds the audience at this "primal scene" is its own watching, sight as it originates in the divided and alien form of the gaze.[11]

And yet, for all the lurid prospects of fragmentation, the play's effects are no less associated with possibilities of marvelous coalescence, the possibility that entire destinies might precipitate. "I knew from the start I was born to answer it," Wilson says. "O cursed spite that ever I was born to set it right," says the prince. Wilson's account may suggest something of the grounds for that clairvoyance. With its talk of spells, of unseen transformations, of forcing oneself into another's life in ways that one could not have guessed, Wilson's dedicatory epistle about a moment of interpretive crisis is also, of course, a love letter. Or, rather, it contains that mixture of rivalry and seduction that energizes and delineates a male literary community in the making. "Though I did not know it, my spiritual condition was critical, not to say dangerous, a condition in which a man becomes converted, falls in love, or gives way to mania for wild speculation. In a sense all three destinies awaited me."[12] In love with the play, with the activity of the critic, with the noble, Laertian adversary? One can't quite tell.[13]

In other words, *Hamlet* is, in some basic way, about the workings of interpellation, the experience of being called into a symbolic destiny. In that sense, the overmastering effects of the dumb show should be read less in terms of the specular mechanics of an easily localizable disciplinary regime [14] than in relation to the more sweeping form of solicitation that is at the center of Hamlet's ostentatious mystery and evident from the play's first words: "Who's there?" The retort, "Nay, answer me," is that of the audience: "No, we ask that of you, you reply." As the Ghost does for Hamlet, so the play assumes for its audience an irreducibly questionable shape, that is, mysterious, open to question, but also opening the very prospect and circuit of the question by posing the audience as the elusive answer to its query as much as it poses itself as the answer to theirs.[15] To attend to that strange hailing, to sense the play anticipating or gazing back at us, is to feel the more comforting distances and ratios of historicist inquiry waver and dissolve.

An elaborate set of historical transformations is involved in the passage from the shrill anxieties caused by the catamitical stage to Wilson's genteel community of men of letters, not the least being the emergence of the categories of the "literary" on the one hand and of the "homosexual" on the other.[16] And yet, it is no coincidence that all those historical possibilities converge upon the scene of one man penetrating another at the ear.[17] What is the relation between the odd erotic specificity of that scene of auditory captivation and the conditions for symbolic interpellation in general?

Bearing out claims made for the play by such critics as Francis Barker and Terry Eagleton, *Hamlet* enacts the advent of—calls forth —a modern subject, or what has been described as the liberal, proto-Kantian subject.[18] In the process, the play reveals much about the precise sexual and political underpinnings of that familiar being. The homosocial calculus toward which the play works, a structuring associated with the contractual subject, devolves from a more archaic structure of political and erotic incorporation; the play intimates the erotic prehistory of modern economic subjectivity. And yet the recursive wiles of the dumb show already suggest what makes a generative account of that modern subject problematic, for the play's staging of subjective advents is itself a function of the reflexive being that such a staging seeks to encompass and describe. In that sense the radical historic and epistemological grounds of the subject must ultimately be sought just where the play itself fails as a signifying structure. That limit of symbolic interpellation is suggested by what is perhaps the oddest feature of the scene of auditory captivation: its dumbness.

I

Slight as the moment is, Claudius's belated response to the dumb show is indistinguishable from *the* question of the play, or at least the question that has obsessed modern criticism: the question of Hamlet's delay. To broach that question, one can turn to the First Player's speech, a set piece that situates the scene of interpretive outrage in relation to the play's preoccupation with the reiterative cycles of revenge. Hamlet's emergence from those blind, determinately oedipal coils and his re-articulation as a "new" subject, amounts to a simple shift in his relation to what divides and arrests him.

In the First Player's declamatory account of Pyrrhus "couched in th'ominous horse," "horridly trick'd / With blood of fathers, mothers, daughters, sons"—"heraldy more dismal"—Hamlet might recognize the densely figured image of the tyrant he must overcome, the bloody and oedipally mired avenger he must become, but also, as critics have suggested, the paralysis that stays his hand.[19] "Hellish Pyrrhus" encounters the ancient King Priam:

> Anon he finds him
> Striking too short at Greeks. His antique sword,
> Rebellious to his arm, lies where it falls,
> Repugnant to command. Unequal match'd,
> Pyrrhus at Priam drives, in rage strikes wide,
> But with the whiff and wind of his fell sword
> Th' unnerved father falls. [Then senseless Ilium,]
> Seeming to feel this blow, with flaming top
> Stoops to his base, and with a hideous crash
> Takes prisoner Pyrrhus' ear; for lo his sword,
> Which was declining on the milky head
> Of reverent Priam, seem'd i' th' air to stick.
> So as a painted tyrant Pyrrhus stood
> [And,] like a neutral to his will and matter,
> Did nothing. (2.1.468–82)

As an account of auditory capture, the scene recalls the dynamics played out at the dumb show; the bloodied tyrant reinforces our suspicion that it is not oversight or calculation that suspends Claudius at the moment of truth. But "Pyrrhus' pause" (2.2.487), the interval during which the tyrant "d[oes] nothing," also recalls Hamlet's inaction, of course.

Why does Pyrrhus pause? The scene lends itself to a Girardian reading of revenge and its inherent contradictions. In his overmastering power, the tyrant swings wide and misses the ancient king altogether. As the passage continues, that excessive and reverting violence is recast in the form of a castrating split within the avenger's own will, a neutering of desire that leaves the tyrant momentarily indistinguishable from the "unnerved father" (2.2.474). For René Girard, the suspension of the act and the convergence of identities between tyrant and victim would be bound up equally with the originative nature of the violence enacted. To the extent that the revenger is engaged in an inaugural act of differentiation, to the extent, that is, that the paternal object was never anything more than a ghost figure, the revenger's decisive action will always amount to a renewed self-violence. The more he seeks to constitute himself, the more he reiterates an originative split within himself; the more he asserts difference from the object of revenge, the more he effaces difference.[20] To cast that paradox in Freudian terms, the suspension of the tyrant's blow would thus be emblematic of a genre in which the conflation of paternal and usurping roles in the figure of the adversary forces into view a fatal redundancy inherent in oedipal desire as such.[21] When it comes, the violence of the revenger will always be exorbitant, stoked, like Claudius's outrage, by its own self-subverting contradictions.

Hamlet's decisive intervention in the reiterative mechanism of revenge entails a simple shift in his relation to that neutering pause. As Wilson has observed, "Hamlet returns from his voyage a changed man, with an air of self-possession greater than at any other time in the play."[22] The "new" Hamlet crystallizes in a single line he speaks upon his return. When Horatio tells Hamlet that the King will soon learn of the execution of Rosencrantz and Guildenstern, Hamlet replies: "It will be short; the interim's mine, / And a man's life's no more than to say 'one' " (5.2.73–74). In sending the messengers to their death, Hamlet produces a deadline for himself: he must act before the returning message betrays what he knows of the king's intentions and the desperate measures he has therefore undertaken. If the constitutive violence directed against the other merely reverts against the revenger, the reverting act—the act whose consequences are willingly drawn down on one's own head—lets the revenger force his own hand and thus constitute himself indeed. The apparent simplicity of that reversal and the anticipatory space it opens must not obscure its resonance in the play. The "interim" that Hamlet speaks of is the split and pause that haunt the male revenger's act, now miraculously transformed into the enabling measure of his life.

To understand the significance of Hamlet's all-important claim that the interim is his own, consider the prince's modern equivalent, another famous model of autochthonic subjectivity: Harold of *Harold and the Purple Crayon.* In this children's book, Harold is a boy who draws his own story as he goes along—the house he wakes in, the path he walks, the adventures he encounters, even his bedcovers at the end. Can Harold draw everything? He can draw the world, the sun and moon, his parents. Can he draw himself? Yes, except for a tiny remainder, a fragment of the hand or crayon that does the drawing. Hamlet's returning message—"Rosencrantz and Guildenstern are dead" (5.2.371)—corresponds to that inassimilable residue, Harold's crayon, or, according to another lexicon, the Lacanian *objet petit a,* the constitutively missing object in the formation of subjectivity and desire.[23] It is at once the most inconsequential line in the drama (one thinks, "What is *that* doing in the midst of this great denouement?") and the most significant, the remainder that has brought about the close and constituted the hero. For Hamlet to come into his own does not mean abolishing that surplus. More significantly, it means being able to acknowledge its space or interim as his very condition. "I can not live to hear the news from England," Hamlet says in his dying speech, a line whose symbolic weight is measured precisely by its remarkable gratuity (5.2.354).

What allows the passage from blind reiteration to comprehension?

What lets Hamlet compass rather than reenact division now as a defining interval? One can begin to recognize the significance of the action Hamlet undertakes aboard ship by considering an interesting contradiction in the psychic posture he displays on his return. On the one hand, as critics have noted, Hamlet reveals a new resoluteness, a stark, oppositional aggressiveness quite distinct from the rusing indirections of the old Hamlet.[24] Hamlet announces his return: "High and mighty, You shall know I am set naked on your kingdom. To-morrow shall I beg leave to see your kingly eyes" (4.7.43–45). The emergence of that agonistic relation between mirroring adversaries reflects the general turn in the play from Oedipal entanglements to an overlapping series of homosocial bonds, each structured, as such identificatory or mimetic bonds always are, around an arbitrarily excluded third. The mixture of rivalry and idealizing identification in Hamlet's relation to Laertes ("by the image of my cause I see / The portraiture of his" [5.2.77–78]), the fact that such a specular pairing is forged within the grave of the woman they passed between them, the emergence in the final scenes of a displaced homophobic object in the person of the effeminate courtier, Osric, all amount to the multiple and telltale indicators of a homosocial structuring of desire, an articulation initiated by Hamlet's fateful actions during the shipboard passage.[25] Hamlet's justification for dispensing with the hapless messengers—"'Tis dangerous when the baser nature comes / Between the pass and fell incensed points / Of mighty opposites" (5.2.60–63)— barely conceals the fact that it is the sacrifice of the intermediaries, their reduction to the status of insinuating go-betweens, that resolves the mighty opposites into mighty opposites.

On the other hand, it would be just as correct to say that the transformed Hamlet is defined not by a new resolve but by a new equanimity, even a passivity: "There is special providence in the fall of a sparrow. If it be [now], 'tis not to come; if it be not to come, it will be now" (5.2.219–23).[26] The play moves from a dispensation of blood revenge to a staged duel, from blindly rivalrous captivation to a specular encounter where one knowingly takes on one's fate in the acknowledged form of a game in which one might equally have played the part of the other; Hamlet does, after all, represent Claudius in the final wager.[27] If attempting to come into one's own through direct confrontation only produces a paralyzing ensnarement, a certain slackening indifference—the ability to acknowledge that one is a function of a supervening mechanism—seems to precipitate a resolution.

Contradictory as those equally necessary postures may seem, they converge in, or emerge out of, the single act Hamlet undertakes aboard ship. At once a suicidal gesture—a self-abnegation—and the sacrifice that establishes the possibility of an identificatory consolidation, the death of the messenger ultimately founds the possibility of Hamlet's identification not with another but with his own negation. As paradoxical and intricately orchestrated as that identification with nonidentity may seem, it is also fundamental and quite familiar, for it amounts to the condition for emergence of a definitively phallic subjectivity. Ultimately, Hamlet's saving identification is not with the specular, homosocial adversary but with the elusive, purely negative function that defines them both, that enables and derides every possible identity. "I'll be your foil, Laertes," Hamlet says (5.2.255). As Lacan implies, it is not mimetic rivalry but the irreducible relation between negation and affirmation implicit in Hamlet's pun—to deny the adversary is also to set him forth in his true splendor—that makes this final play of foils a phallic encounter.[28] Hamlet's witty acknowledgment of his own negative condition here at the end should not obscure the force that underwrites such an insight; if that definitive, always elusive negative term is able to come to light at all, it is only by virtue of the act of violence that has allowed it to become for Hamlet the locus of his own identity.

Such phallic identification underlies the distinctive cast of knowingness that characterizes the hero at the end, a knowingness all the more powerful for its knowing it does not know. The specular nature of the final confrontation does nothing to diminish the fact that Hamlet remains fated to miss his own destiny. By the time he looks without for what threatens, it has already passed within.

> Hamlet:  O villainy! Ho, let the door be lock'd!
> Treachery! Seek it out.

Laertes:   It is here, Hamlet. Hamlet, thou art slain.

    ·  ·  ·  ·  ·  ·  ·  ·  ·  ·  ·  ·

The treacherous instrument is in thy hand. (5.2.311–16)

The reversions and belatedness of the dumb show continue to the end, making Hamlet's decisive encounter with his own limit, in Lacan's terms, an "encounter forever missed."[29] And yet Hamlet knowingly takes on such a condition now, insofar as he enters the final game as a game, insofar as he enters it on the wrong side as his own foil, as it were, and insofar as he approaches all toward the end within the compass of an inarticulable foreboding: "Thou wouldst not think how ill all's here about my heart—but it is no matter" (5.2.212–13). If the tyrannical revenger's act merely reinscribes his division and blindness, Hamlet's fateful accession confirms him as the one who already knows he is blind.

The knowingly unknowing—absorbed and foreseeing—subject that emerges from the point of Hamlet's return and that is so calculatedly staged against the prospect of reiterative captivation resonates well beyond the context of revenge drama and its impasses. The "new" Hamlet amounts to a harbinger of the modern, Kantian subject, a subject explicitly articulated around its own formal limit, whose knowledge remains "no matter," a matter, that is, of pure negation. The historical coordinates of that negative subject become apparent when the play's most striking formal feature—the fact that it is structured around the hero's disappearance, his brief shipboard passage beyond the gaze of the audience—is understood as the literary equivalent of the pictorial vanishing point, that empty point in symmetrical relation to which a uniform subject coalesces for the first time.[30] The slightly comic fact that it is to England that Hamlet disappears —as if the hero vanishes by moving toward the theatrical audience, comes into view by receding—merely confirms how precisely the subject within such a symbolic dispensation is structured around its own eclipse.

Punctiform and abstract, that matterless subject is nonetheless also a distinctly economic being. The scenes that follow Hamlet's return are marked by the emergence of a discourse of class, again figured in the person of Osric, the "water-fly" courtier who is as socially deracinated as he is genderless. Discursive groundlessness, the madness that possessed the prince himself, is now thematized as an economic phenomenon. Hamlet mocks the newly made man's linguistic excesses, his tendency to speak "sellingly"—"to divide him inventorially would dozy th' arithmetic of memory"—and to spend himself discursively—"His purse is empty already: all's golden words are spent" (5.2.109, 113–14, 130–31).[31]

But it is not just Osric who is conceived economically. Hamlet himself completes his destiny within the terms of a wager. The phallic identification that is the key to Hamlet's "turn" at the end is also the condition for the emergence of a specifically economic subject, understood as function of circulation and exchange. Nor should we underestimate the salutary nature of such an economic identification, whatever the era's laments against the commodification of the self. The resolution of *Hamlet* turns on the transition from blind inscription within a reiterative cycle to a saving capacity to comprehend oneself as a mere factor or substitute within a circuit of exchange.

As one might expect, the formal, proto-Kantian subject has recognizable political coordinates as well, a fact most evident at the point where Hamlet in fact confronts his limit. "O, I die," Hamlet says at the end,

> I cannot live to hear the news from England,
> But I do prophesy th' election lights
> On Fortinbras, he has my dying voice.
> So tell him, with th' occurrents more and less
> Which have solicited—the rest is silence. (5.2.354–58)

Hamlet's otherwise improbable foreknowledge of the improbable fact that the English messengers will arrive at the same moment as the new heir suggests how much all at play's end is governed not by verisimilitude but by the demands of a more fundamental symbolic logic. Index of his subordination to the signifier, the interval by which Hamlet falls short of his own returning message, and thus falls short of himself, is also the measure of his inscription within the supervening political domain of election and succession.

The entire tragedy—the "occurrents more and less"—is now subordinated to the task of negotiating that interim as an interim, of conveying Hamlet's voice to the successor it will designate. And yet, the status of that all-important "dying voice" remains tellingly unclear. Acting at once as what prophesies the successor and what elects him, Hamlet's voice causes what it foresees. This paradox reflects Denmark's status as an elective monarchy, a mixed form in which a vestige of lineal power is preserved in the form of prophetic knowledge. At the same time, the elective prophecy equally anticipates a contradiction at the heart of the liberal subject, a subject defined by its freely contractual relation to the political/symbolic domain.[32] That subject's voice is at no point more powerful than at its death; indeed, it is predicated on death, for it is only in relation to its own limit that the subject can be said to have an autonomous, elective voice, a voice that extends beyond it. The "mouth whose voice will draw on more" is the mouth whose voice will draw no more (5.2.362). But precisely because it is founded on death, because it harbors death as its prior condition, the elective voice must have exceeded such a limit from the outset. Like the foreboding prince, the modern and contractual subject is from the beginning a subject that knows too much, knows more than it can know.[33]

## 3

To claim, however, as has often been claimed, that *Hamlet* marks the determinate origin of a discrete historical subject—the liberal subject, the Kantian subject—overlooks precisely what is most vexed about such an emergence. To problematize such a developmental account one must return to the vanishing point, the fateful action that Hamlet undertakes aboard ship, and comprehend what that act signifies for Hamlet: that is, an accession to the symbolic order as such. The mixture of unmediated spontaneity ("Or I could make a prologue to my brains, / They had begun the play" [5.2.30–31]) and simulation (the "play," as it turns out, involves forging the messenger's death warrant) that defines Hamlet's decisive action on the ship crystallizes in the gesture with which he seals the letter that seals his unsuspecting companions' fate, as well as his own.

> Horatio: How was this seal'd?
> Hamlet: Why, even in that was heaven ordinant.
> I had my father's signet in my purse,
> Which was the model of that Danish seal. (5.2.47–50)

Hamlet here takes on the paternal signifier—assumes his "proper" identity—for the first time, but he takes it on explicitly in its capacity as a simulacrum or "model."[34]

One might read Hamlet's divinely ordained recourse—again, an identification with nonidentity—in terms of his personal development; through such a diminishment of the paternal function to an empty signifier—its true, ghostly status—Hamlet is able to release himself from the snares of oedipal identification that have bound him thus far. One might also see Hamlet's decisive use of the counterfeit seal in historical terms, that is, in relation to what Richard Halpern sees as the transition from a sovereign or juridical model of cultural inscription based on law and transgression to a civil or bourgeois model based on the proliferation of systems of self-fashioning and on the ascendence of *imitatio* as a pedagogical method.[35] Hamlet himself presents his use of the "fair" hand that lets him mime sovereign authority as recourse to a bureacratic skill he had once abjured.

But neither of these developmental accounts recognizes what is problematic about symbolic inscription as an "event." In fact, the truth of Hamlet's accession is only revealed after the fact, after his own demise, at the point at which the message returns. The English ambassador arrives too late:

> Ambassador: The sight is dismal,
> And our affairs from England come too late.
> The ears are senseless that should give us hearing,
> To tell him his commandment is fulfill'd

> That Rosencrantz and Guildenstern are dead.
> Where should we have our thanks?
> Horatio:                                         Not from his mouth,
> Had it th' ability of life to thank you.
> He never gave commandment for their death.
>
> (5.2.367–74)

Horatio is speaking of Claudius here, of course. But the sustained, indefinite "he" at this point produces a momentary confusion: Didn't he—Hamlet—give the commandment?[36] However fleeting, the interpretive lapse is significant. It represents the closest thing to a symbolic fulfillment in the play, for it is only here, through misrecognition, that Hamlet finally assumes his regal identity. Further, though, the misrecognition may be unresolvable. The more one deceives oneself by "leaning" on one's knowledge of Hamlet as the guilty author of the missive in order to assure one's own, sovereign textual posture beyond the counterfeit, the more one brings to view the true, limitless nature of that counterfeit. In fact, Hamlet never gave the order of death; it did not arise from his mouth, nor any living mouth, but from the point of his submission to the empty paternal signifier. Rather than being a determinate moment, symbolic accession—the "seal" of sovereign identity—is thus shown to have the performative, implicative status of what Lacan terms a "*point de capiton*," the always retroactive, always misrecognized *après coup* through which any symbolic field is sealed and made signifiable.[37]

Hamlet comes into his own beyond himself, at the unrecoverable point at which his identity merges—has always already merged—with the limitless counterfeit of the play itself. Hamlet can at best be said to mark the advent of a subject that, to invoke the elliptical temporality peculiar to the symbolic register, will have already occurred. Does the metaleptic, always missed nature of that symbolic accession and its convergence with the play's own expansive textuality subvert any effort to conceive its limits? Not necessarily. It does suggest that one look to the conditions of that subjectifying mechanism as a mechanism, which means turning to the figure who is buried, not merely barred, before the play resolves.

The lyricism of the Queen's account of Ophelia's exquisite demise, that narrative's status as a "pastoral" interlude in the serious, head-long drama, should not obscure the fact that it presents a significant counterversion of Hamlet's own destiny and of the entire mechanism of symbolic interpellation articulated around his disappearance and return:

> There is a willow grows askaunt the brook,
> That shows his hoary leaves in the glassy stream,
> Therewith fantastic garlands did she make
> Of crow-flowers, nettles, daisies, and long purples
> That liberal shepherds give a grosser name,
> But our cull-cold maids do dead men's fingers call them.
> There on the pendant boughs her crownet weeds
> Clamb'ring to hang, an envious sliver broke,
> When down her weedy trophies and herself
> Fell in the weeping brook. Her clothes spread wide,
> And mermaid-like awhile they bore her up,
> Which time she chaunted snatches of old lauds,
> As one incapable of her own distress,
> Or like a creature native and indued
> Unto that element. But long it could not be
> Till that her garments, heavy with their drink,
> Pull'd the poor wretch from her melodious lay
> To muddy death. (4.7.166–83)

Like Hamlet, Ophelia is shown to exceed her own limit by the briefest interval, to remain, like the tyrant, oddly suspended at the moment of truth. And again that surplus—what remains of the subject beyond the subject—is affiliated with the fact of symbolic inscription. The voice continuing beyond the mind's power to conceive, the woman drawn "from her melodious lay / To muddy death" as if it were the song itself that had miraculously sustained her: these are the signs of the "floating signifier," the signifier in excess of the being it animates. And, if we can judge from the aside about "liberal shepherds" with their "grosser nam[ing]," which ruffles the chaste surface of the pas-sage, here, too, symbolic accession can be associated with the gross intrusion of the phallic function. And yet, the scene shows what Hamlet's accession does not: not only is the interim not one's own, but if it sustains at all, it is only in the form of an impossibly precarious living death—a form of madness.

What keeps Ophelia afloat? To answer that, one must examine Ophelia's death scene in relation to a contradiction at the heart of the phallic subject as articulated in *Hamlet*. If it is the exclusion of the third that enables the emergence of an identificatory relationship, how can that third—the empty, purely negative term—ever itself become the object of identification? And if that term cannot be conceived in terms of object identification, how does the subject accede to symbolization? Ophelia suggests an answer. Against all those agonistic, specularized relations between men that structure the conclusion of the play can be set the fleeting image of the willow showing itself to the "glassy stream." Here, too, the interim, the space beyond, is bound up with a moment of identification, but here a specular moment strangely antecedent to any viewer.

That agentless reflection—figure for Ophelia's own suspended status beyond her end—can be understood in relation to the "enigmatic, pre-objectal identification," which Julia Kristeva associates with the boundaries of symbolization. For Kristeva, the emergence of signification is bound up with a fragile interspace between an originary autoeroticism, in which a distinction between subject and object has yet to appear, and the advent of object cathexis, which is to say the advent of desire, under the aegis of paternal prohibition and the oedipal complex. What sustains that space? Narcissism, Kristeva suggests, but a specular narcissism prior to the subject it supports and whose object is no object but emptiness—the gap or interim that founds the possibility of signification. "Narcissism protects emptiness. . . . Without that solidarity between emptiness and narcissism, chaos would sweep away any possibility of distinction, trace and symbolization, which would in turn confuse the limits of the body, words, the real, and the symbolic."[38] At its limit, the subject is what Ophelia amounts to in her floating interlude: an empty mirroring, a specular mirage suspended against dissolution.

Ultimately, Ophelia is not, or not merely, the barred figure supportive of the male, identificatory relations that emerge at the close; Lacan's remarks to the contrary, she is not the phallus.[39] Instead, she represents the suppressed face of the entire mechanism of subject formation as it is played out at the end of *Hamlet*. By the same token, Ophelia's death scene also suggests that the interim that founds signification is itself an improbably fragile structure, an emptiness in need of bolstering, and thus that symbolic inscription is anything but an irreducible or inescapable mechanism. Does Hamlet, the "sovereign" subject of the play, confront that prospect—not the castrating returns of symbolic inscription but a more radical faltering of symbolization? The play at least seems to open that possibility, and it seems to do so, paradoxically, at the point at which Hamlet encounters the paternal function most directly. "What if it tempt you toward the flood . . . And draw you into madness?" Horatio says of the returning ghost (1.4.69,74).

## 4

Why should an encounter with the father, even a dead father, amount to an encounter with madness? The performative nature of the Ghost's appearance, the fact that it cannot be separated from the act of recounting it, even from the punctual returns of theater itself, suggests that the dead father is bound up with the workings of the symbolic register as such. If the Ghost returns even to those whose ears are "fortified" against his return, if it haunts, it is because it represents the indissociable relation between denial and affirmation, abjury and conjury peculiar to the symbolic order.[40] And yet, to align the Ghost with the paradox of constitutive lack explains neither his power to solicit nor the fantasy his return enacts. The truly startling prospect opened by the Ghost is not that one might be able to hear stories about the other world but that one might be able to complete one's own. The Ghost's fantastic and entirely unnecessary account of the poison's passage inward through the ear and veins simply metaphorizes the thrillingly impossible subject position that every ghost opens, the prospect that one could witness the moment of one's own death.

If the conclusion of the play is oriented around the possibility of comprehending one's own limit as limit, of knowing one doesn't know, the encounter with the Ghost opens the even stranger possibility that the limit might be abolished altogether. And that way madness lies.

One cannot complete one's own story, of course; even ghosts can't, apparently. The moment of completion slips away in the minute ellipsis between a figure and its application. "In the porches of my ears" was poured the "leprous distillment,"

> whose effect
> Holds such an enmity with blood of man
> That swift as quicksilver it courses through
> The natural gates and alleys of the body,
> And with a sudden vigor it doth posset
> And curd, like eager droppings into milk,
> The thin and wholesome blood. So did it mine,
> And a most instant tetter bark'd about,
> Most lazar-like, with vile and loathsome crust
> All my smooth body. (1.5.63–73)

"So did it mine": The "encrusted," alien body may itself be taken as figure for the loss entailed in that always belated recognition that one was already caught up in a figure, already inscribed. Suggesting the connection between ear poisoning and the forgery through which Hamlet will take up his sovereign identity, the Ghost says

> 'Tis given out that, sleeping in my orchard,
> A serpent stung me, so the whole ear of Denmark
> Is by a forged process of my death
> Rankly abused. (1.5.35–38)

And yet, the vile, fascinating "bark'd" body, congruent in its strange appeal with the armored emptiness that speaks, clearly entails something quite distinct from the exacting, formal seal—the paternal signifier—that Hamlet takes on at the end, something closer to the "coagulate gore" that defines Pyrrhus's feudal "heraldy more dismal" (2.2.462, 456).

To understand the peculiar erotic density of the specter's returning body, one must recognize where the fantasized threat it poses is situated. If loss insists in this case, it is a loss returning beyond loss, beyond the proscribed limits of castration and death that structure and sustain the symbolic order. In that sense, the Ghost hearkens beyond castration to a more archaic accession. At its most primitive, Kristeva suggests, at the level of primary identification, access to the symbolic is bound up with the oral drives: one "swallows" the signifier of the other to assimilate a model of the self. That is in part what is so disquieting about the Ghost's metaphor of ear poisoning, the implication that language might be ingested, that it might have the status not of pure lack but of thing.[41]

Indeed, that strange, erotically freighted non-object—language as thing—has its equivalent in the Lacanian lexicon in *das Ding*. Irrupting beyond the dialectics of symbolic negation, *das Ding* or *l'extimité* represents in the Lacanian account a more radical breach within being —a "strange body in my interior which is 'in me more than me,' which is radically interior and at the same time already exterior," the intimate body as "lazar-like" crust.[42] Though consisting of nothing other than the phenomenon of its own infraction, that inward and alien body nonetheless assumes the resonance of an inert, inassimilable "thing" insofar as it amounts to the limits of symbolic negation. And, though it is no more than its infraction, the splitting it entails hearkens beyond the regulated play of prohibition and desire implicit in symbolization to the workings of the death drive. Fulfilling the Lacanian dictum that "desire itself is a defense," *l'extime* amounts, in Žižek's words, to "a hard core embodying horrifying *jouissance* . . . and as such an object which simultaneously attracts and repels us— which divides our desire."[43]

"What, has this thing appear'd again to-night?" (1.1.21). When Hamlet proclaims, "The king is a thing . . . of nothing," he articulates a fundamental insight about the symbolic status of sovereignty, not that the King is insignificant but that he is sovereign—the anchor of the entire political and symbolic field—to the extent that he is nothing, to the extent that he embodies pure negativity. Hamlet's riddle, "The body is with the King, but the King is not with the body" (4.2.27–28), registers the paradox of a form of symbolic surplus that is at once the measure of the King's lack and source of his intangible power. But that recognition about the King's constitutive nothingness is set against another possibility. What the Ghost exposes, and what Hamlet must forget, is that if the King is a thing of nothing, he remains a thing nonetheless; the body is not with the King, and yet even at its most spectral the sovereign body retains an erotic undertow and density.

That erotic force may not be separable from what seems most strange about the monarch's body as it was once conceived: the fact that it was not just a political body but a body politic. Modern theorists generally present the "organic" theory that the polity inheres within the person of the king as a self-evident ideological fiction, an effort to naturalize the social field that would be demystified only with the emergence of modern theories of political representation. Such a view fails to recognize that the very notion of the state is as an abstract entity; indeed, the notion of the symbolic domain as a distinct and purely formal category is a historical one.[44] In *Hamlet,* hearkening beyond such a separation, the King's archaic, charismatic body implies something more than a simple naturalizing of the social: it opens the more unsettling prospect that the symbolic register itself—the law as such—might retain an untoward erotic charge.

In other words, the "body politic" may well have had a libidinal life of its own. In terms of subject formation, such an eroticized conception of the political anatomy means taking the idea of incorporation as something more than an opportunistic metaphor. Before and beyond the negative, reasoning, inscribed subject of civil society, one should imagine an incorporated subject constituted as both inward and alien, a political *extime* of sorts.[45]

*Hamlet* stages the emergence of the "autonomous" subject against the imagined horizon of a more archaic and more luridly conjured social formation—the passage, that is, from incorporation to paternal inscription, from coagulate "heraldy" to sovereign signifier and seal. That passage is not, strictly speaking, a chronological one. Neither, however, is it reducible to the model of a supervening textual mechanism, the signifier's pure and limitless returns. It should be sought rather in the difference between what recurs within symbolization "as such" and what returns from beyond, between the return of the repressed and a more radical and phantasmatic foreclosure. Ophelia's death should be understood in relation to the articulation of that difference. Even with its own sacrificial victims, the disappearance and return that inaugurate the phallic prince as a symbolic subject — that inscribe him — remain inadequate. Beyond the pure negativity of symbolization, a more thoroughgoing exclusion is required in order to constitute the paternal demand as a purely symbolic injunction and to constitute the symbolic order itself — the domain of law — as a purely formal space. Ophelia "answers to" the law, responds to but also appeases and allays its extravagant undertow, what arises at the point where symbolization brushes up against the death drives.

At the level of sexual economy, the tentative nature of that social/symbolic transformation is evident in the fragility of the distinction between the homosocial bond — those structures that inscribe the subject at the purely formal level of exchange — and an eroticizing of the paternal function itself; mingled with the taint of maternal orality, the Ghost's overdetermined fantasy of ear poisoning carries with it a residue of anal jouissance, dreadful insofar as it communicates beyond the prohibitory father of symbolization.[46] For Hamlet, the unstable nature of that boundary becomes evident at the murkiest level of his actions aboard ship, a level where the erotic aim of his entire passage and return seems to waver between bodies and the letter of the law:

> Up from my cabin,
> My sea-gown scarf'd about me, in the dark,
> Grop'd I to find out them, had my desire,
> Finger'd their packet, and in fine withdrew
> To mine own room again. (5.2.12–16).

Elide the boundary between the homosocial and pre-oedipal jouissance completely, and homosociality passes into the truly strange, which is to say truly pre-modern, reaches of the same-sex theory, a masculinist construction for sure, but one whose conviction that one sex is no more than the unbroken inverse of the other, that female genitals are male genitals turned inside out, seems to bypass the structuring function of castration altogether and fulfill the logic of incorporation in its most intimate form.[47]

All of which leads back to the scene of interpretive outrage and its erotic contours. Suggesting as it does an extravagantly inward communion of minds, the image of one man penetrating another at the ear conveys, under the aegis of oedipal aggression, all the idealizing force of the homosocial bond. Even at its most hyperbolic—perhaps especially at its most hyperbolic—outrage can function to sustain such a mimetic, communal bond. But one can also detect a less recuperable erotism in the scene of penetration, the suggestion of an odd convergence of aural and anal registers, as if the paternal function—symbolization itself in all its coursing, quicksilver purity—harbored an unthinkable material and sexual trace.

What form does that poisonous trace assume for the auditor? Something about the extradiegetic set pieces discussed earlier troubles the purity of their seemingly boundless mirror effects: precisely their failure to bear out Hamlet's own mimetic ideal of "suiting word to action, action to word."[48] While the dumb show presents a silent image of auditory capture, the First Player's narrative involves an auditory capture that transforms its listener into a silent tableau—a painting. More than specular captivation is entailed in that chiasmus between hearing and sight. Figured within the First Player's narrative by the fleeting moment in which "senseless Ilium" captures the ear and in which the listener is threatened with inanimateness, the passage into mute audition amounts to an instance of identification, but an exorbitant, nonmimetic identification that passes beyond the oedipal frame and undoes the very distinction between sensible and insensate, living and dead.

"The ears are senseless that should give us hearing," the Ambassador announces on his interpellating return (5.2.369). The form of dumb audition evoked in the First Player's speech suggests that one seek out the "grounds" of the subjectivity that the play calls forth beyond the neutering pause of castration and the boundless negativity of language—its performative entrapments—in a more rudimentary and unstable rhetorical moment. As Cynthia Chase argues, the specularity inherent in any text's recursive, self-referential effects cannot in principle be distinguished from the radically arbitrary and immediate identificatory act through which one determines that such effects are signified *there,* within the text. Rhetorically, that act amounts to an instance of prosopopoeia, the bestowal of face and signifying status on the sheer, "senseless" material of signification—language, not as a field of signs but as "indeterminably significative gestures or marks."[49] Significantly, in *Hamlet* that signifying limit, the mark of absolute contingency, coincides with the point at which the subject is articulated directly in relation to history, to the event that marks the mythic advent and end of England as a nation: the fall of Ilium.[50]

The ear-poisoning scene implies a taint within the speculative subject, a taint that suggests the limit of an entire sexual and political articulation; in that scene, homosocial exchange converges on anality, inscription on incorporation. Ultimately, however, such accounts thematize a more radical horizon of legibility. Limitlessly performative as *Hamlet* is, the sheer performativity of the play is not what disquiets. The real scandal is precisely that such a reading of the play as infinite mediation cannot sustain itself, that something "madding" and intractable "remains," in T. S. Eliot's words, "to poison life."[51] *Hamlet* enacts the emergence of the subject as pure thing of nothing, as performative effect; it also broaches what is inassimilable to such a subject: not the prospect that it might be nothing, but the contingency and thus the radical historicity of that nothingness.

Returning from Troy to Sunderland, one can now see the larger stakes of that scene of reading. Wilson's account of the effect of interpretive crisis suggests the retroactive logic of symbolic interpellation—"capitonage"—in supremely concise form: "I must have read the article a half a dozen times before reaching Sunderland, and from the first realized that I had been born to answer it."[52] We think of Hamlet on the battlements hearing a call that he, too, knows he was born to answer. The dumb show's captivating effects, groundless as they may be, are of a piece with that marvelous, retroactive coalescence, especially insofar as the scene's very emptiness is translatable into a form of unspoken and knowing bond. And yet, to hear *Hamlet*'s "questionable" voice as an answerable voice, to integrate it into a legible, symbolic field, means risking a more exacting solicitation, a dumb, arresting appeal that the play at once broaches and shores against. Muting that mute appeal, forcibly establishing it in some manageable, familial relation to symbolic inscription, amounts to the violently contradictory condition for the always belated emergence of the modern man of letters.

# Chapter 5

# Subject Matter

"How now Ophelia, what's the matter?" (2.1.72); "Now, Mother, what's the matter?" (3.4.8); "What is the matter, my lord?" / "Between who?" / "I mean the matter that you read, my lord" (2.2.193–95); "Thy commandment . . . shall live / Within the book and volume of my brain / Unmixt with baser matter" (1.5.102–4); "Like a neutral to his will and matter" (2.2.481); "This something settled matter in his heart" (3.1.173); "There's matter in these sighs" (4.1.1); "This nothing's more than matter" (4.5.174); "Thou wouldst not think how ill all's here about my heart —but it is no matter" (5.2.212–13).

It is not a coincidence that matter has come so deeply to matter in early modern studies.[1] I now return to one of the questions raised at the outset, the question of the relation between early modern subjectivity and materialism, cultural or otherwise. In some sense, my aim will be to historicize matter; if it's possible to speak of historicizing the subject, it should also be possible to historicize the object or even to historicize materiality as such, matter in its seemingly most irreducible form.[2] At the same time, a historical materialist account of the era will fall short precisely to the extent that it does not account for the obsessive and overdetermined character of matter as an entity or ground, the extent to which it does not lend itself to objectification. Ultimately, the political and historical dimensions of the early modern subject—its relation to a shifting body politic and, especially, the vastly transformative advent of exchange relations— becomes apparent only when one considers just how phantasmatic a thing matter is during the era.

For all that has been claimed for the distinctive character of the Renaissance subject, it might be easier to make a case for early modernity's significance to the genealogy of the object. For, in a certain sense, the object as such, the object in its irreducible material thingness, is an early modern invention. Lorrain Daston traces the derivation of the modern concept of the pure, recalcitrant thing, the object as datum outside any prior structure of intention or interpretation, back to an intriguing middle category of medieval thought, neither the natural nor the supernatural, but the preternatural.

That epistemological twilight zone, Daston argues, consisted of phenomena—prodigies, portents, marvels, monstrous births—that did not conform to the laws of nature but that also did not necessarily or consistently lend themselves to being read as direct expressions of divine will. As such phenomena became affiliated with the demonic during the sixteenth century, the category of the preternatural came increasingly into its own. Because of that association, and as the multiplication of sects increasingly vexed the interpretation of portents, preternatural phenomena tended to be cited without interpretive elaboration, as "singularities" or uncategorizable occurrences. For Bacon, and in the context of an emerging empirical/scientific epistemology, such forms become the guarantors of scientific reason precisely because of their intractability; because it checks or remains unassimilable to prior theoretical supposition, the "deviating instance," as Bacon terms it, becomes something like the pure ground of knowledge. Thus, by the seventeenth century, the fascinating marvel has marvelously transited into the "neutral" fact.[3]

I want to focus on what may be the most intriguing moment in this developmental narrative of the object, the interim between portents-taken-as-signs and the establishment of the neutral facts of scientific reason, between the world of the similitude and that of empiricism, where the thing first appears in all its marvelous illegibility. I explore here that momentarily charged and inscrutable matter in two contexts, one cultural, the other literary, in order to arrive at some broader reflections on the modern subject, including the psychoanalytic subject, and history.

I

To explore the phenomenological status of the early modern object at its most distinctive, I want to begin by looking into the notably odd space of Renaissance wonder cabinets, where collectors gathered the singular things of the world. The *Wunderkammern* has traditionally been taken to represent the object as conceived within a distinctly pre-Enlightenment regime of knowledge. Rather than simply representing a naïve or preliminary gesture toward classification, the cabinet of marvels figured the material object as it was constituted within the vast web of similitudes or correspondences that make up the universe. If the small space of the cabinet can be seen to approximate or even conjure the world, that is because the world is constituted in terms of exactly such metaphorical correspondences between microcosm and macrocosm, man and world, mundane and divine.[4] To the extent that such a metaphorical system amounts to an epistemology, to the extent, that is, that it constitutes the terms of human knowledge, it is never, of course, conceived as merely figurative. "Whatsoever is in the universal world," Nicholas Culpepper writes, "is also in man: not according to a certain superficial similitude as some fools prattle; but in deed and in reality, are contained in him whatsoever is in the whole theater of the world."[5]

Such an account of the wonder cabinets as microcosms explains everything about them except their most salient feature: their preoccupation with precisely what is singular, odd, and unclassifiable, with "the rarity." It is just this prevalence of the anomalous that leads Daston to associate the wonder cabinet with a newer preoccupation with the object as such. Anticipating Bacon's privileging of the deviating instance as a crucial check to the mind's innate tendency to abstract and theorize, the wonder cabinets, in their deliberate severing of syntax—the mummy next to the winged cat next to the horn of the unicorn—demonstrate a dawning preoccupation with the "brute 'thing-ness'" of objects.[6] As if allegorizing such a transitional moment, the 1599 engraving of Ferrante Imperato's museum in Naples produces the impression of things become oddly unmoored from the surrounding library, adrift in an unmapped space above, neither quite the dimensional space of the room, nor the flat space of the page (fig. 23).[7]

But if the wonder cabinet reveals something like the emergence of the "singular instance"—the thing in itself—that possibility in itself does not explain the perhaps prevailing characteristic of these singular forms: their partialness. "In most cases, [the collectors] were dealing not with whole animals but with parts of them, often very small and insignificant parts such as teeth, horns, tusks, nails, feathers, pieces of skin, or bones."[8] This is not just a matter of the difficulty of acquiring whole specimens; as Amy Boesky points out, "most striking" about the list of objects that Tradescant commissions for his burgeoning collection is its active preference for the "dismembered or partial."[9]

Why should the thing in its brute thingness first appear in the form of a *partial* thing, a part-object? The answer lies in the singular object's relation to the seeker of knowledge. The *curieux* was defined at once as one who "pries" into secrets and as one "who enjoys a special relationship with totality." Krzysztof Pomian clarifies the apparent paradox: the collector of curiosities was one who, "dissatisfied with a knowledge of the common and the normal, seek[s] greater knowledge of the singular, and accordingly searches among natural and artistic artifacts for rare, exceptional and extraordinary objects, objects supposed to have a special link with totality as they constitute the source of additional information without which the knowledge of the world as a whole, or one or other of its domains, would remain incomplete."[10] The rarity implies a totality of knowledge insofar as it represents something in addition, a supplement to knowledge. If the valued object itself retains that supplemental form—if it appears as a part-object—that would simply be a measure of the extent to which the object as such, in its singularity, is a function of the limitless desire for something more.[11]

A charmed fragment, a contingent and supplementary form that somehow places the subject in relation to the desired whole, the rarity would seem to be nothing if not a fetish object. The term *fetish*, in both its Marxist and psychoanalytic appropriations, has been the subject of especially energetic historical revisionism in recent years, some

Figure 23. Ferrante Imperato's Museum. Engraving in Imperato,
*Dell'Historia Naturale* (Naples: 1599).

with pertinence for the early modern era. William Pietz argues the term should not be divorced from its etymological derivation from instances of crosscultural mercantilist exchange between Europe and West Africa from the fifteenth century on, exchanges that necessarily entailed an experience of the incommensurable nature of social values.[12] One thinks of the wonder cabinet's curious mix of natural marvels and anthropological plunder.[13]

Still, Pietz's historico-linguistic account could be accused of, well, fetishizing the term: the literality of the analysis of derivations implicitly justifies itself insofar as the fetish is seen to "embody" or reflect the contingency implied by such an approach. Radical historicism in this instance is underwritten by an unspoken rhetorical mimeticism. At the same time, the psychoanalytic account most attuned to fetishisms' rhetoricity suggests an unspoken historical frame of reference, even a horizon of usage, perhaps. Here's Lacan: "The enigmas that desire seems to pose for a 'natural philosophy'—its frenzy mocking the abyss of the infinite, the secret collusion with which it envelops the pleasure of knowing and of dominating with *jouissance,* these amount to no other derangement of instinct than that of being caught in the rails—eternally stretching forth towards the *desire for something else*—of metonymy. Hence its 'perverse' fixation at the very suspension-point of the signifying chain where the memory-screen is immobilized and the fascinating image of the fetish is petrified."[14]

It is worth noting how directly Lacan's analysis of the grounds of desire suggests the distinctive relation between cultural adventurism and knowledge, between burgeoning empiricism—"natural philosophy"—and the fantasy of illimitable expansion crystallized in the Renaissance cabinet of wonders. The "petrifying" dimension of the fetish, as Lacan describes it, is there in the cabinet as well, in oddly literalized form. Consider the striking prevalence in these collections of what were termed *petrifications*—natural matter wondrously turned to stone.[15]

Those forms may vividly figure the (newly) masterful subject's powers to turn the things of the world into the fixed objects of its gaze. But their fuller significance would seem to be bound up with the peculiar hold of the fetish as Lacan describes it. Embodying the supervention of the signifying chain itself in relation to the subjects that chain inscribes, such forms convey the very grounds of fascination in the object's reciprocal capacity to fixate all who gaze on it: consider the severed Medusa-like head in the engraving of Calceolari's cabinet, its gaze stilled but not banished, as well as the multifarious anamorphically distorted faces that populate the space, as if the "object" here amounted to so many reverting and scattered points of subjective identification (fig. 24).[16] That fetishistic reversal is figured in the creature that recurs in these collections with emblematic frequency: the basilisk.[17]

If the early modern "rarity" is something like a fetish, is it of a piece with the commodity, that most famous of modern fetishes? The cabinet of curiosity will indeed eventually become an explicitly bourgeois phenomenon, nature and culture reduced to the blazoned bric-a-brac of a merchant class, and it wouldn't be hard to imagine the cabinet of curiosity in all its scientific pretensions as a space within which the brute thingness of the empirical world is imaginatively subjected to the logic of the cumulable commodity.[18] In that sense the wonder cabinet's collection of natural and artificial oddities amounts to a precursor of, say, the bourgeois still life, the petrifications and monstrous anamorphoses of the one paradoxically anticipating the exquisite opacity of the other, those hypnotizing surfaces through which the captivations of the gaze are endlessly and mutely renewed by the very sheen that seals the object-form within itself.[19]

Still, something about these collections remains inassimilable to a logic of bourgeois accumulation, even to the metonymic logic Lacan describes in relation to the fetish. To perceive that something, one might consider the wonder cabinet in relation to another moment in the Lacanian analytic, a passage in which he describes the signifying dimension not in its relation to metonomy and desire but in relation to what Freud describes as the incorporative function of mourning.[20] In a reading of *Hamlet*, Lacan writes: "What are these rites [of mourning] by which we fulfill our obligation to what is called the memory of the dead—if not the total mass intervention, from the heights of heaven to the depths of hell, of the entire play of the symbolic register . . . for it is the system of signifiers in its totality that is impeached

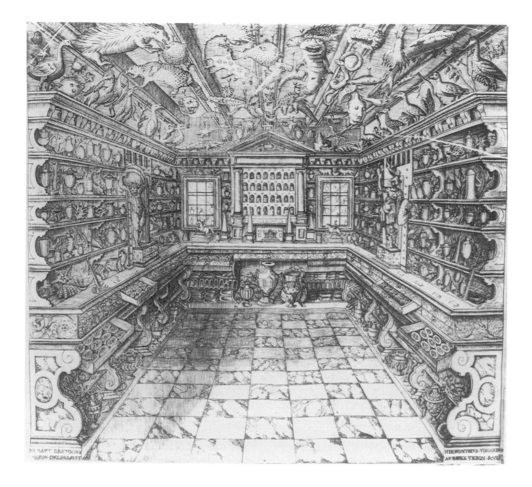

Figure 24. The Museum of Francesco Calceolari. Engraving in B. Ceruti and
A. Chiocco, *Musaeum Francisci Calceolari* (Verona, 1622).

by the least instance of mourning."[21] With its reference to the totality of the symbolic order, mourning here resonates with the incorporative logic behind the cabinet of the world, with its vast system of magically embedded similitudes.[22] Indeed, with their countless mummies and petrifications, their shells and "amber wherein were several insects intomb'd," these spaces feel closer to the mausoleum than the shop or the boudoir, as if the fantasy of metaphorical incorporation also implied a scene of encryption, and as if the things of the world were being shored against a more extravagant emptiness than the lack that propels the acquisitive bourgeois subject.[23]

Consider what makes the 1580 engraving of *Metallotheca*—Michele Mercati's museum of rocks, minerals, and fossils—striking (fig. 25). The image vividly suggests the association between the curiosity cabinet and the Renaissance memory theater; looking again at those architectonically delineated spaces full of natural oddities, one might recall the mnemnotician's preference for the grotesque image, as if the empirical object emerged in the form of the mind's "inner talismans" severed from their defining grid, allegories without ground or reference.[24] But if the Calceolari illustration suggests a memory theater with its inner talisman's cut adrift from any syntax, the Mercati image suggests the more disquieting prospect of a syntax without a subject, as if in the era of the humanist subject, that subject's place might be most vividly felt in the eeriness of a system of similitudes operating around a void. If, as Pomian suggests, the origin of the collection should be understood in terms of a subtractive logic—that is, the sacred and the rare being those objects withdrawn from the circuit of exchange—the universal collection, which is to say the truly marvelous collection, may well be the one which incorporates everything except, of course, a subject.

One might understand the early modern rarity in all its hieroglyphic fascination, then, as the index of a significant historical intersection, the juncture between a metaphorical universe structured around an economy of incorporation or encryption, and a metonymic and specifically empiricist universe in which phenomenal particularity is bound up with the headlong deferrals of the signifying chain. But to describe such a juncture as a historical moment in any simple narrat-

Figure 25. Engraving of Michele Mercati's *Metallotheca*
(Museum of Minerals and Fossils) (1580: published in Mercati,
*Metallotheca. Opus Posthuman*) (Rome: 1717).

able sense is problematic. For it amounts to the intersection between two infinitudes: first, a metonymic chain that is illimitable or that, according to the logic peculiar to the symbolic register, will have already been in place; and second, an instance of incorporation that nevertheless includes that signifying dimension in its totality. To situate the marvelous, uncategorizable "singularity" there would be to see it in all its specificity as an impossible object, a kind of historical phantasm.

2

To explore the implications such an object—what appears fleetingly in the gap between the worlds of similitudes and facts—has for my conception of an equally transitional subject, I turn from the objects in the cabinet to the subject in the closet, a famous subject in a famous closet. The "closet scene" in *Hamlet* has assumed its hypnotizing privilege for modern, psychoanalytic accounts of the male subject by virtue of its lurid oedipality, of course. In the play's own terms, the scene is critical in that it is the one in which the famous prince finally speaks the famous truth he has harbored, the truth of the crime: Hamlet's is nothing if not an epistemological closet. But the closet is also an anatomy theater of sorts, as Michael Neill has observed;[25] the scene, like the play, is no less preoccupied with matter, as its opening suggests: "Now, Mother, what's the matter?" (3.4.8). And in the end, it yields up matter—a body, a body that seals the play's course and the male hero's fate. In a world of words, Polonius's opaque body seems to retain the rare, galvanizing power of the irreducibly brute thing.[26] What is the relationship between the subject in the closet and the body in the closet, between subject and matter? And how does that matter matter for modern accounts of the subject?

> Hamlet: Come, come, and sit you down, you shall not boudge;
> You go not till I set you up a glass
> Where you may see the inmost part of you.
> Queen: What wilt thou do? Thou wilt not murther me?
> Help ho!

Polonius:                   *[Behind]* What ho, help!

Hamlet:     *[Drawing]* How now? A rat? Dead, for a ducat, dead!

              *[Kills Polonius through the arras.]*

Polonius:    *[Behind]* O, I am slain.

Queen:                 O me, what hast thou done?

Hamlet:    Nay; I know not, is it the King?

Queen:     O, what a rash and bloody deed is this!

Hamlet:    A bloody deed! almost as bad, good mother,

            As kill a king, and marry with his brother.

Queen:     As kill a king!

Hamlet:               Ay, lady, it was my word.

*[Parts the arras and discovers Polonius.]*

Thou wretched, rash, intruding fool, farewell!

I took thee for thy better. (3.4.18–32)

Why does Hamlet speak his great truth at this moment? The scene might be read as an affirmation of unthinking impulse—"praise be for rashness."[27] Hamlet is able to enact here blindly what he cannot act with calculation and in performing the deed—or what he takes to be the deed—is finally able to articulate the crime that drives him. Still, the gesture of stabbing through the arras would seem to engage in a more precise way the play's thematics of secrecy and voyeuristic intrusion; by slaying the interloper, the shadow presence that in the porous world of the play has always stolen the prince's words from him, Hamlet is finally able to speak directly and truly.

But who, exactly, is the "rash intruding fool"? Claudius's spy, of course. Claudius himself, perhaps—the figure who has "popp'd in between th'election and [his] hopes" (5.2.65). Reading the scene as oedipal fantasy, it would be the ghostly father himself that Hamlet imagines intruding on the maternal scene. Even Gertrude might be taken for the interloper, judging from Polonius's words to her: "Your Grace hath screen'd and stood between / Much heat and him"; certainy there is enough of the matricide in Hamlet's behavior during the scene to suggest that she is the fantasized object of violence. Given the dramatized intimacy of the scene, and thus the exquisite heightening of identificatory attention, one could even say that it is the audience itself that finds itself oddly inscribed in the role of the "rash, in-truding fool," riven by its own voyeuristic absorption, its unflagging desire to lay bare what it already knows.

Most significantly, however, it is Hamlet himself who functions as screen and go-between here. What is one to make of the curious pause, of a piece with the prince's famous delay throughout, between Hamlet's stabbing through the arras and his lifting it to reveal the body, the interval within which he speaks his secret truth? It is not sufficient to say that Hamlet is protecting himself against his own knowledge that the body is not the king's: he is quite explicit about his doubts on that score. In a more radical sense, the hesitation should be seen to open a space for the entire range of phantasmatic possi-bilities. In other words, Hamlet's pause is what reveals the scene to be a scene of fantasy, taking fantasy in its precise psychoanalytic ac-ceptation not as an imagined object of desire but as the frame which structures the very possibility of desire and its objects.[28]

Hamlet's gesture of sustaining the arras he rends is of a piece with the most striking feature of the scene generally: its ostentatious re-dundancy. The exchange between mother and son amounts to a sus-tained echolalia.

Hamlet:   Now, mother, what's the matter?
Queen:   Hamlet, thou hast thy father much offended.
Hamlet:   Mother, you have my father much offended.
Queen:   Come, come, you answer with an idle tongue.
Hamlet:   Go, go, you question with a wicked tongue.
Queen:   Why, how now, Hamlet?
Hamlet:                 What's the matter now?

(3.4.8–14)

A tight-lipped defense against intimacy, or Hamlet's aggressive sign that he knows his most private words are not his own? In fact, the scene elides any easy distinction between privacy and exposure. The exchange climaxes when Gertrude takes Hamlet's promise to "set [her] up a glass / Where [she] may see the inmost part of [her]" as a threat: "What wilt thou do? Thou wilt not murther me?" Is the murderous danger here exposure, or the more extreme prospect that the empty specularity of the exchange might take in everything? "Now, mother, what is the matter?" The matter, the scene suggests, is precisely that the matter—the substance of desire and meaning—approaches the perfect, killing emptiness and redundancy of the maternal circuit: "Mater, what is the matter?"[29]

One needs an altogether different vantage point, a position outside, even to see the "mother" as the "matter," to bring her into view simply as the ground of the question of desire. According to the familiar Lacanian schema, it is the intervention of the third—the paternal function—that breaks the stupefying circuit of pre-oedipal captivation and opens the path of desire for the first time. And, indeed, after Polonius's intercession, matter—a tangible body—precipitates from the scene, a body that Hamlet will cling to as if it were the substance of his being.

But where, exactly, does that seemingly irreducible matter come from? Polonius is first conjured as both a voice from outside and an extension of the chiasmic returns from within:

Queen:     Help ho!
Polonius:  [Behind] What ho, help!

Is Hamlet's violence intended to protect the space of maternal discourse from an intervention, a shielding that constitutes that space as a space of desire for the first time? Or, does matter fall out only by virtue of a fixative violence directed against discourse itself in all its ramifying exorbitance, a violence against "maternal" discourse that will return in the form of discursive violence against the mother: "My words are daggers." Is it the protective arras or the dagger that constitutes the possibility of object-desire? To the extent that the entire scene is a function of address, to the extent that it is purely discursive, the two gestures—sustaining the arras, breaching it—may in fact be indistinguishable. An effect of the limitless and purely negational field of the signifier, desire in this "primal" scene would amount to a constitutive and entirely reiterative violence, a rending that produces what it violates.

Understood thus, the body in question, the matter that so fixates attention, is purely tropic. Indeed, the violence that yields up the body can be seen to inscribe the audience within the play's well-known "tropical" mouse—or rat—trap." A rat? Dead, for a ducat. "In his edition of *The Hystorie of Hamlet*, Horace Furness writes of *Hamlet*'s relation to its source: "Amidst all the resemblances of persons and circumstances, it is rather strange that none of the relater's expressions have got into [Shakespeare's] play; and yet not one is to be found except in Act III, where Hamlet kills the counsellor . . . behind the arras . . . and is made to cry out: 'a rat, a rat.' "[30] It is just at the point where reference is violently fixed, where the recursive play of tropes is arrested and matter forced, that the play accedes most directly to the illimitably textual economy within which it is inscribed.

Does this tropic account exhaust the matter of matter in the scene, or even the matter of the mother? Elsewhere, another maternal figure momentarily arrests the prince, a figure at the almost forgotten margins of the oedipal drama. After Polonius interrupts the First Player's set-piece of the starkly oedipalized encounter between ancient, overmatched Priam and Pyrrhus, with its own violence and its own castrating pause—"Like a neutral to his will and matter" (2.2.481)—Hamlet intervenes: "Say on, come to Hecuba." That figure of mourning at the edge of the agonistic scene prompts a more fleeting arrest:

Player:     But who, ah woe, had seen the mobled queen—
Hamlet:    "The mobled queen"?
Polonius:   That's good, "mobled queen" is good. (2.2.501–4)

Tempting as it might be to hear in the "mobled" or "muffled" queen a voice from beyond the closet wall, a substantive possibility beyond the staging space of fantasy, even beyond the terms of the play, to do so would be to reiterate Hamlet's pinioning violence and thus to be reinscribed within the play's textual economy. But if the prince is momentarily held by the "mobled" queen, it is neither necessarily because of that figure's referential claims nor because of its place within language understood as a system of tropes. Indeed, within the line's tightly wound chiasmic turns—"who, ah woe," "seen the . . . queen"—the antique neologism *mobled* can be seen to figure precisely what remains inassimilable to language as trope, that is, its own sheer positedness as signifier, its dumbness.[31]

Situated at the intersection between desire and mourning, the mute remains of the incessant talker—matter as such in the play—may retain something of the arresting force of the "mobled" queen. The body arises as an effect of the fixating reduction of desire in the scene, but also as what remains impervious to and thus precipitates from the entire frame of fantasy and desire. The obsessiveness of *Hamlet's* relation to matter, as well as the implied relation between matter and madness, derives from that equivocality that places matter both in and beyond fantasy, in and beyond desire, and thus in and beyond the entire scene of "discovery" within which early modern knowledge is inscribed. The hysterical nature of Hamlet's response to the corpse, the insistence with which he alternately clings to and distances himself—and the king—from it suggests not just the magnetizing properties of the fetish but a hectic effort to reestablish the very intervals of desire and signification.[32]

Significantly, for Hamlet that struggle translates directly into a political recognition. Asked to bring the body to the king, Hamlet replies:

| Hamlet: | The body is with the King, but the King is not with the body. The King is a thing . . . |
| Guildenstern: | "A thing," my lord? |
| Hamlet: | Of nothing. (4.2.27–30) |

The "moral" of this exchange is familiar: to know that the corpse exerts a power somehow beyond itself, that matter at its most irreducible is a function of a signifying mechanism that exceeds it, is also to know that the King is a thing of nothing, that he at once falls short of and goes beyond any empirical manifestation insofar as he is king, insofar as he embodies the social and symbolic field as such. And yet, if the thing can be nothing, doesn't that also imply the perhaps more troubling inverse: that nothing—the pure abstraction of the body politic—might be a thing, of sorts?[33] Polonius's body sets in motion a radically democratic fantasy in which political and symbolic incorporation becomes indistinguishable from excretion:

Hamlet:   A man may fish with the worm that hath eat of a king,
          and eat of the fish that hath fed of that worm.
King:     What dost thou mean by this?
Hamlet:   Nothing but to show you how a king may go a progress
          through the guts of a beggar. (4.3.27–31)


3


The queasily direct passage from body to body politic in the play suggests again how closely the play's psychic embroilments are related to the historical moment of an ambiguous and as-yet fragile individuation of a subject on the one hand and an abstract "state" on the other. That political/historical moment is, the closet scene suggests, a matter of signification, or the subject's relation to the limits of signification as such. Hamlet's account of political incorporation may help us recognize how directly the epistemology of matter—the wondrous singularity, the excrescency—is bound up with structural transformations in the social domain.

In language wonderfully apt for *Hamlet*, Richard Halpern describes the effects of a drastically changing polity:

> If merchant's capital brought about a primary decoding of late feudal production in order to recode it in the sphere of exchange, the vagrant poor represented an absolute decoding, the decisive separation of the producer from the means of production. The dispossessed classes had a strong anticipatory force; by "mirroring" the decoding effects of capital in a way that overstepped the structural limitations of late feudal production, they became a precocious and nightmarishly exaggerated image of *modernity*. They were a kind of volatile fluid coursing irregularly through the social body and visible everywhere in it, representing the possibility of a total and anarchic breakdown of the existing mechanisms of order and control.[34]

The phenomenon of vagrancy—the "masterless man" so endlessly and luridly evoked in contemporary accounts—takes on its overdetermined character insofar as it appears as a kind of phantasmatic revenant and precursor within the body politic, as what is unsignifiable within the social reality it at the same time enables.

These are men not matter. But we can recognize the force and significance of the connection by considering Marx's structural account of the historical transition Halpern describes, the transformative passage into exchange relations. Marx repeatedly observes that the process of abstraction that yields exchange value entails an intractable "residuum," a "congealed mass" or "coagulated jelly." For Marx, that residue is significant: it amounts to what has been critically repressed from all modern accounts of economy and exchange value, what he terms "undifferentiated human labour."

Why does human labor assume that strange form in Marx's account, a "phantom-like objectivity" and a "congealed mass" in a process that nevertheless "leaves not an atom of matter behind"?[35] Thomas Keenan associates such matter with what he takes to be the critical aporia in Marx's account of the advent of the exchange relation. As Marx makes clear, "use-value," often assumed to be the substantive ground for exchange value, is itself irreducibly contingent: it has no determinate form or being in its own right. For it to arise at all, then, exchange requires its own structuring term, an abstract term of comparison comparable to the oedipal "third" in order to establish the possibility of similitude out of the sheer heterogeneity of use. Where does that founding term come from? From the process of abstraction itself, paradoxically enough. Marx's account of the commodity is underwritten by a kind of "ghostly matter," in Thomas Keenan's account, amounting at once to an "ineffaceable excess"—"the oddly material if nonsensible 'jelly' of a remnant that resists incorporation [into exchange]"—and to "the condition of possibility for the operation that must already have happened in order to leave it behind."[36] Matter in its most irreducible form is, for Marx, the residue of the process it allows, which is to say spectral through and through.

"Coagulate jelly," "ghostly matter": it is not hard to hear in all this the volatile, intractable stuff that courses through king and state in *Hamlet*. Reading Marx's account of advents historically, one could say that the matter that haunts early modernity and early modern subjectivity is neither a sign nor an empirical instance but a phantasmatic effect of the passage between social and symbolic epochs, that which is conjured in the interval between the dissolution of the corporate body politic and the emergence of a society structured around the exchange relation.

That is an indeterminable—belated, anticipatory—event, but perhaps picturable nonetheless. Consider Willem van Swanenburgh's 1593 woodcut, not of a wonder cabinet, but of an anatomy theater, another early modern space that amounted at once to a "museum, a mausoleum, and a theater," as Amy Boesky observes (fig. 26).[37] It was a commercial site as well, judging from the practice of selling tickets to the spectacular displays, which would draw hundreds and often go on for days.[38] Like the cabinet, the anatomy theater—here, the famous one at Leiden—inscribes the empirical gaze within an older, metaphorical universe, with the microcosmic body of man now explicitly laid out as the center and reference point of the concentrically ramifying universal theater. The emblematic status of the dissection scene is here signaled by the prominent tableau of the two skeletons dioramically enacting the fall in the foreground.[39] As with other engravings of anatomy theaters, something of the relationship between incorporation and specular reversal is visible in the whimsical motif of the specimens as theatrical onlookers, the risk of absorption smuggled in within the terms of the older memento mori tradition.

Most significant for my purposes, though, is the small group of figures at the periphery of the scene, two men and a woman gazing at and passing between them a fabric-like skein: to the side of the metaphorical anatomy, a small tableau of exchange—a woman between men, an object in circulation. What is significant, of course, is the nature of that object—not material but a human skin—and its relation to the main scene; if the group at the margin might be seen to figure a different social and symbolic economy, the exchange relation in place of the corporate body, the object that structures such an economy is in this instance nothing more than the fascinating residue of that body, a formless form without a determinable place inside or outside the body proper. Isn't that anamorphic form something on the order of the "phantom-like" matter that recurs in Marx's account, at

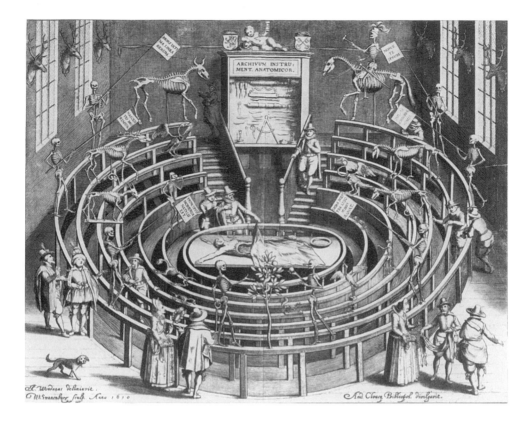

Figure 26. *Anatomy Theater*, by Willem van Swanenburgh (after an engraving by J. C. Woudanus) (1593). Reproduced with permission of the Academisch Historisch Museum, Leiden, The Netherlands.

once the eviscerated, disincorporating effect of the exchange relation itself—its residuum—and the prior, spectral ground of the relation?

To associate matter with that groundless ground is to suggest in its most immanent and human form what makes disincorporation so significant and problematic as a historical moment. Claude Lefort describes the radical "opening" that accompanies the dissolution of the "organic" social body. What emerges, he writes, is a society "that has become the theater of an uncontrollable adventure, so that what is instituted never becomes established, the known remains undermined by the unknown, the present proves to be undefinable, covering many different social times which are staggered in relation to one another within simultaneity—or definable only in terms of some fictitious future; an adventure such that the quest for identity cannot be separated from the experience of division. This society is *historical* society *par excellence.*"[40]

Is the early modern thing constituted within historical society, does it occur "in" history? Or is it what allows that "adventure" and temporal opening in the first place? Walter Benjamin remarks that for the late Renaissance history as such assumed the form of "a petrified primordial landscape," a collection of things;[41] as if inscribed within the indeterminate continuities of a Möbius strip, pursuing the thing within history may mean finding history elsewhere, in the thing.[42] At the same time, insofar as it poses the question of history, the thing also poses the question of the subject. If the modern subject, the psychoanalytic subject as well as the commodified one, must be understood within the context of the fundamentally historical "quest for identity" that Lefort describes, what does it mean that that subject is nevertheless limned by the trace of that which one can't even designate simply as prior, that which precipitates from and enables historical society and historical subjectivity?

"Between the acting of a dreadful thing / And the first motion, all the interim is / Like a phantasmata, or hideous dream" Brutus says before his fateful action against the body of the state.[43] To recognize the phantasmatic nature of such an interim, and to feel its resonances with Hamlet's more famously suspended act, one must read it not as the space between thought and action, as many an editor has, but as an undoing of the act as such.[44] The oedipal dimensions of such a moment are evident enough. But one might also read that hallucinatory interval in relation to the interim of early modernity itself, a belated, anticipatory space between political and symbolic universes within which a certain subject and a certain historicity appear. In that sense, "phantasmata"—matter's phantasmatic ground—broaches the fundamental relation between the speculative subject of modernity, the subject as "thing of nothing," and its unspoken, enabling human and economic detritus.

# Notes

## Introduction

1 Francis Barker, *The Tremulous Private Body: Essays on Subjection* (London: Methuen, 1984), 37.

2 Ivo Kamps, ed., *Materialist Shakespeare: A History* (London: Verso, 1995); Valerie Wayne, ed., *The Matter of Difference: Materialist Feminist Criticism of Shakespeare* (Ithaca, NY: Cornell University Press, 1991); Linda Charnes, *Notorious Identity: Materializing the Subject in Shakespeare* (Cambridge, MA: Harvard University Press, 1993).

3 Wayne, *Matter of Difference,* 7.

4 Jonathan Dollimore, *Radical Tragedy: Religion, Ideology, and Power in the Drama of Shakespeare and His Contemporaries,* 2d ed. (Durham, NC: Duke University Press, 1993), 249–50.

5 Margreta de Grazia and Peter Stallybrass, "The Materiality of the Shakespearean Text," *Shakespeare Quarterly* 44 (1993): 256, 257, 280.

6 Margreta de Grazia, Maureen Quilligan, and Peter Stallybrass, eds., *Subject and Object in Renaissance Culture* (Cambridge: Cambridge University Press, 1996), 4.

7 Elizabeth Hanson, *Discovering the Subject in Renaissance England* (Cambridge: Cambridge University Press, 1998), 16. Katharine Eisaman Maus offers an equally probing account of the significance of inwardness as a category in the early modern era in *Inwardness and Theater in the English Renaissance* (Chicago: University of Chicago Press, 1995).

8 Hanson, *Discovering the Subject,* 2–3, 17.

9 Ibid., 25.

10 Ibid., 11–12.

11 Jean Howard, "The New Historicism in Renaissance Studies," *English Literary Renaissance* 16, no. 1 (1986): 18, 25.

12 Stephen Greenblatt, "Psychoanalysis and Renaissance Culture," in *Literary Theory/Renaissance Texts,* ed. Patricia Parker and David Quint (Baltimore: Johns Hopkins University Press, 1986), 218.

13 Ernesto Laclau, *New Reflections on the Revolution of Our Time* (London: Verso, 1990), 3–33, 89–92.

14 Karl Marx, *Collected Works* (London: Lawrence and Wishart, 1976), 3: 167. For an especially rich account of the ramifying emergence of the state in England during the sixteenth century (from 1530), see Philip Corrigan and

Derek Sayer, *The Great Arch: English State Formation as Cultural Revolution* (Oxford: Blackwell, 1985), esp. 43–71, 166–80.

15  Claude Lefort, *The Political Forms of Modern Society: Bureaucracy, Democracy, Totalitarianism*, ed. John Thompson (Cambridge: MIT Press, 1986), 186–87.

16  *Ibid.*, 201, 222. Corrigan and Sayer speak of the sixteenth-century emergence of "society as such" within the English context (*The Great Arch*, 106).

17  William Shakespeare, *The Tempest*, ed. Hallet Smith, in *Riverside Shakespeare*, ed. G. Blakemore Evans et al. (Boston: Houghton Mifflin, 1974), 3.2.135–43.

18  Jacques Lacan, "The Subversion of the Subject and the Dialectic of Desire," in *Ecrits: A Selection*, trans. Alan Sheridan (New York: Norton, 1977), 292–324.

19  Slavoj Žižek, *The Sublime Object of Ideology* (London: Verso, 1989), 87–89.

20  Elizabeth J. Bellamy, *Translations of Power: Narcissism and the Unconscious in Epic History* (Ithaca, NY: Cornell University Press, 1993), 1–37. Also see Timothy Murray's fine introduction to *Repossessions: Psychoanalysis and the Phantasms of Early Modern Culture*, ed. Timothy Murray and Alan K. Smith (Minneapolis: University of Minnesota Press, 1998).

21  Stephen Greenblatt, "Psychoanalysis and Renaissance Culture," 216.


## 1. The Theater, the Market, and the Subject of History

1  Jean-Christophe Agnew, *Worlds Apart: The Market and the Theater in Anglo-American Thought, 1550–1750* (Cambridge: Cambridge University Press, 1986), 42.

2  *Ibid.*, 112–13.

3  Don Wayne, "Drama and Society in the Age of Jonson: An Alternative View," *Renaissance Drama* 13 (summer 1982): 128, and Karen Newman, "City Talk: Women and Commodification in Jonson's *Epicoene*," *English Literary History* 56 (summer 1989): 506.

4  On economic discourse as an organizing feature of New Historicism, see H. Aram Veeser's introduction to *The New Historicism*, ed. H. Aram Veeser (New York: Routledge, 1989), xiv–xv.

5  Stephen Greenblatt, *Shakespearean Negotiations: The Circulation of Social Energy in Renaissance England* (Berkeley: University of California Press, 1988), 155.

6  *Ibid.*, 19.

7  William Shakespeare, *Henry VI, Part 1*, ed. Herschel Baker, in *The Riverside Shakespeare*, ed. G. Blakemore Evans (Boston: Houghton Mifflin, 1974),

1.4.39–41. All subsequent references to Shakespeare's plays in the chapter will be to this edition and will be cited parenthetically within the text.

8 See Christopher Pye, *The Regal Phantasm: Shakespeare and the Politics of Spectacle* (London: Routledge, 1990), 18–23.

9 The relationship between the autonomous workings of exchange and the return of the dead is echoed in Philip Stubbes's invective against usury: "It is as impossible for any to borrowe money there [in the market] without . . . some good hostage, gauge, or pledge, as it is for a dead man to speak with audible voice" (*The Anatomie of Abuses*, ed. Arthur Freeman [1583; reprint, London: Garland Press, 1973], K$^v$r). To recognize the unspoken fear, just invert the analogy: raising the dead may be as easy as borrowing money. Death itself is not "gauge or pledge" enough against the exorbitance of exchange. From the point of view of the subject, the death drive coincides with the point of expenditure without return, an uncanny space "beyond the personal and the social," which William Flesch beautifully explores under the term "extremity" (*Generosity and the Limits of Authority: Shakespeare, Herbert, Milton* [Ithaca, NY: Cornell University Press, 1992], 12–21).

10 The ventriloquistic apostrophe that allows the hero to assume his destiny by assuming the place of the dead in symbolic form only, even as it founds the symbolic order in all its autonomous potency—"wretched shall France be only in my name"—on a phantasmatic form of specular identification, represents theater's ideological function in its most irreducible form: a violently repercussive misreading, but a misreading that constitutes the possibility of meaning; a repression, but a repression that conjures what it excludes. My account of Pucelle's function in the scene is not incompatible with Leah Marcus's suggestive argument that she represents a "distorted image" of England's own martial maid, Queen Elizabeth I, and thus taps the gender anxieties associated with female rule. See *Puzzling Shakespeare* (Berkeley: University of California Press, 1988), 51–83.

11 The scene thus bears out Homi Bhabha's argument that the homogeneous, "continuist" temporality of nationalist narrative is forged on the active forgetting of the "ghostly time of repetition," a "zone of occult instability" prior to the founding of a determinate "national will" ("DissemiNation," in *Nation and Narration*, ed. Homi K. Bhabha [New York: Routledge, 1990], 295–310).

12 According to the *O.E.D.*, "centure" means "girdle," thus bringing to mind the site of the theater just beyond London's walls. I am indebted to Scott McMillin for the insight about the audience's uncertainty about its location at this point in the play.

13 Jacques Derrida, "*Fors:* The Anglish Words of Nicolas Abraham and Maria Torok," trans. Barbara Johnson, in Nicolas Abraham and Maria Torok, *The*

*Wolf Man's Magic Word*, trans. Nicholas Rand (Minneapolis: University of Minnesota Press, 1986), xiv. For a sophisticated reading of Abraham and Torok's theory of "cryptation" in relation to the gender-specific foundations of Renaissance autobiography, see Timothy Murray, "Translating Montaigne's Crypts: Melancholic Relations and the Sites of Altarbiography" in *Repossessions: Psychoanalysis and the Phantasms of Early Modern Culture*, ed. Timothy Murray and Alan K. Smith (Minneapolis: University of Minnesota Press, 1998).

14 William Shakespeare, *Richard II*, ed. Herschel Baker, in *The Riverside Shakespeare*, ed. G. Blakemore Evans (Boston: Houghton Mifflin, 1974), 1.4.39–41; *Henry IV*, ed. Herschel Baker, *Riverside Shakespeare*, 3.2.143–50.

15 The relationship between economy and revenge is evident in the fear, and the reassurance, each occasioned. The fear is that a human institution can assume a life of its own: the limitless circuits of exchange, the limitless cycles of revenge. The reassurance: precisely that the mechanism is self-sufficient, thus localizable and capable of being known.

16 That the specular metaphor functioned within economic thought as much as economy functioned within theater is evident in this climactic passage from Edward Misselden's *The Circle of Commerce*, the first English treatise to theorize economy as a fully autonomous function:

> It is said of *Sapor* King of *Persia*, that he carried a great globe to be made of Glasse, of such curiosity and excellency, that himself might sit in his throne, and he and it, in the *Center* thereof, and behold the motions and revolutions of the Starres, rising and falling under his feet: as if he that was a mortall man, would seem immortall. And surely if a King would desire to behold from his throne, the various revolutions of Commerce, within and without his Kingdome; he may behold them all at once in this Globe of glasse, *The Ballance of Trade*. For indeed if there bee any vertue in the Theorick part of Commerce, that might attract a Princes Eie to be cast upon it; surely it is in this kind of *Exchange*, that one Country maketh with another in the *Ballance of Trade*. . . . All the waight of Trade falle's to this *Center*, and comes within the circuit of this *Circle*. . . . This is the very Eie of the Eie; or it is the pupill or apple of the Eie, or as the *Rabbins* calle it, the daughter or image in the Eie. (*The Circle of Commerce* [1623; reprint, New York: Augustus Kelley, 1971], 141–42.)

Rather than undoing it, the notion of economy as a global function reinscribes sovereignty, not as the fixed term or ground of exchange but as a specular reflection of the totality of the system itself. Although he speaks exclusively of the balance of trade, Misselden's elaborate optical and monarchic fantasy should be seen as the antecedent to any effort to elevate exchange "as such" to a sovereign term. Whether it is the subject who discovers his weakness in the shaming effects of commodification or the sovereign who discovers his omnipotence reflected back in "the Eie of the Eie" of exchange, the economic register is bound up with the empty, sustaining returns of the specular relation.

17 On the association, see Agnew, *Worlds Apart*, 40.

18 Michel de Certeau, *The Writing of History*, trans. Tom Conley (New York: Columbia University Press, 1988), 5.

19 Wlad Godzich, "In-Quest of Modernity," foreword to Michael Nerlich, *Ideology of Adventure: Studies in Modern Consciousness, 1100–1750,* trans. Ruth Crowley (Minneapolis: University of Minnesota Press, 1987), 1: xi–xii.

20 I am not proposing an argument against periodization; for there to be disruption, there must be a structure in place to be disrupted. Instead, I am suggesting that to ignore history's dislocations—the fact that in quite determinate ways history fails—is to ignore the specific locus of subject formation. For the argument that the subject is inevitably a function not of social structures but of their failure to constitute themselves as totalities, see Ernesto Laclau, *New Reflections on the Revolution of Our Time* (London: Verso, 1990), 40–41.

21 Thomas Nashe, *Pierce Penniless's Supplication to the Devil* (1592; reprint, London: Shakespeare Society, 1842), 59–60.

22 "I will defend [plays]," Nashe continues, "against anie collian, or club-fisted usurer of them all, there is no immortalitie can be given a man on earth like playes. What talke I to them of immortalitie, that are the onely underminers of honour, and doo envie any man that is not sprung up by base brokerye like themselves?" (60).

23 David Miller, *The Novel and the Police* (Berkeley: University of California Press, 1988), 26–32.

## 2. Froth in the Mirror: Demonism, Sexuality, and the Early Modern Subject

1 Stephen Greenblatt, *Shakespearean Negotiations: The Circulation of Social Energy in Renaissance England* (Berkeley: University of California Press, 1988), 1.

2 The best known version of conjuring through inverse writing occurs, of course, in Christopher Marlowe's *Doctor Faustus.*

3 Greenblatt, *Shakespearean Negotiations*, 94–128; Alan Macfarlane, *Witchcraft in Tudor and Stuart England: A Regional and Comparative Study* (London: Routledge and Kegan Paul, 1970), 190–99; Keith Thomas, *Religion and the Decline of Magic* (New York: Scribners, 1971), 493–501, 546–69;

Catherine Belsey, *The Subject of Tragedy: Identity and Difference in Renaissance Drama* (London: Methuen, 1985), 185–91; Peter Stallybrass, "Macbeth and Witchcraft," in *Focus on* Macbeth, ed. J. R. Brown (London: Routledge and Kegan Paul, 1982); Karen Newman, *Fashioning Femininity and English Renaissance Drama* (Chicago: University of Chicago Press, 1991), 53–70.

4 John Cotta, *The Triall of Witch-craft* (1616; reprint, Amsterdam: Da Capo, 1968), 69.

5 Johann Weyer, "*De praestigiis daemonum,*" in *Witches, Devils, and Doctors in the Renaissance: Johann Weyer,* De praestigiis daemonum, ed. George Mora, trans. John Shea (Binghamton, NY: Medieval and Renaissance Texts and Studies, 1991), 429, 431.

6 George Gifford, *A Dialogue Concerning Witches and Witchcraftes* (1593; reprint, London: Oxford University Press, 1931), F4.

7 Greenblatt, *Shakespearean Negotiations,* 105–6.

8 On the relation between witch prosecution and Protestant interiorization, see Stuart Clark, "Protestant Demonology: Sin, Superstition, and Society, 1520–1630," in *Early Modern European Witchcraft: Centres and Peripheries,* ed. Bengt Ankarloo and Gustav Henningsen (Oxford: Clarendon, 1993), 65–77. For a reading of witchcraft as symptomatic of the vexed relation between mind and body during the Reformation, see Lyndal Roper, "Exorcism and the Theology of the Body," in *Oedipus and the Devil: Witchcraft, Sexuality, and Religion in Early Modern Europe* (London: Routledge, 1994).

9 Cotta, *Triall of Witch-craft,* 115.

10 *A true and particular observation of a notable piece of witchcraft practised by John Samuel, . . . Alice Samuel, . . . and Agnes Samuel . . . of Warboys* (1589); reprinted in *Witchcraft,* ed. Barbara Rosen (New York: Taplinger, 1972), 258.

11 *Ibid.,* 263.

12 On witchcraft and hysteria, see Catherine Clément, "Sorceress and Hysteric," in Hélène Cixous and Catherine Clément, *The Newly Born Woman,* trans. Betsy Wing (Minneapolis: University of Minnesota Press, 1986).

13 John Stow, *Annales of England* (1600); reprint in Rosen, *Witchcraft,* 308–9.

14 Cotta, *Triall of Witch-craft,* 114.

15 "The 'crisis of order' historians have recognized in early modern England, and particularly the challenges to traditional ideals of womanhood posed by the proliferation of printed books and increased literacy, as well as by demographic changes bringing about out-of-town apprenticeships or 'service' and later marriage for women, led to the displacement of anxiety onto the woman. . . . The consequence was the criminalization of women" (Newman, *Fashioning Femininity,* 57–58). See also Christina Larner, *Witchcraft and Religion: The Politics of Popular Belief* (Oxford: Basil Blackwell, 1984), 45–46, 58–67, 84–94; and Clarke Garrett, "Women and Witches: Patterns of Analysis," *Signs* 3 (1977): 461–70.

16 Thomas, *Religion and the Decline of Magic,* 559–60.

17 *Ibid.,* 554–69.

18 On witchcraft as *crimen exceptum,* see Larner, *Witchcraft and Religion,* 29–30, 35–67.

19 Ernesto Laclau and Chantal Mouffe, *Hegemony and Socialist Strategy: Towards a Radical Democratic Politics* (London: Verso, 1985), 128–29. For Laclau and Mouffe's account of the necessity of "abandoning, as a terrain of analysis, the premise of 'society' as a sutured and self-defined totality," see 111–14. Although she goes on to emphasize the multidetermined, rather than the overdetermined, character of the witchcraft phenomenon, Robin Briggs's analogy is to the point: "Once we start aggregating, the variables multiply so fast that chaos theory, with its patterns of unpredictability, is the scientific model which best fits the case" ("'Many Reasons Why': Witchcraft and the Problem of Multiple Explanation," in *Witchcraft in Early Modern Europe,* ed. Jonathan Barry, Marianne Hester, and Gareth Roberts [Cambridge: Cambridge University Press, 1996], 53).

20 "The manner of the voice out of the child: the lips moved with none such moving as could pronounce the words uttered" (*The disclosing of a late counterfeyted possession by the devyl in two maydens within the Citie of London* [1574], in Rosen, *Witchcraft,* 237). For Lacan's most condensed account of the subject as function of the signifier, see "The Subversion of the Subject and the Dialectic of Desire," in *Ecrits: A Selection,* trans. Alan Sheridan (New York: Norton, 1977), esp. 303–10. On the association between exorcism and theater, see Greenblatt, *Shakespearean Negotiations,* 106–14.

21 Reginald Scot, *The Discoverie of Witchcraft* (1584; reprint, New York: Dover, 1972), 17. On the witch's mark as a distinctly early modern preoccupation, see Brian Levack, *The Witch-Hunt in Early Modern Europe* (London: Longman, 1987), 46. See also, Thomas, *Religion and the Decline of Magic,* 445–46.

22 On the satanic compact, see Thomas, *Religion and the Decline of Magic,* 439–44, and Levack, *The Witch-Hunt in Early Modern Europe,* 32–35.

23 King James I, *Daemonologie,* in *Minor Works of King James VI and I,* ed. James Craigie (Edinburgh: Scottish Text Society, 1982), 23.

24 Robert Muchembled, "Satanic Myths and Cultural Reality," in Ankarloo and Henningsen, *Early Modern European Witchcraft,* 139, 144. On the relation between the witch craze and the emergence of the modern state, see also Levack, *Witch-Hunt in Early Modern Europe,* 89–90, and Philip Corrigan and Derek Sayer, *The Great Arch: English State Formation as Cultural Revolution* (Oxford: Blackwell, 1985), 64.

25 On the king's double body generally, see Ernst Kantorowicz, *The King's Two Bodies: A Study in Medieval Political Theology* (Princeton: Princeton University Press, 1957); on the relation between the king's body and the state, see Quentin Skinner, *The Foundations of Modern Political Thought,* (Cam-

bridge: Cambridge University Press, 1978), 2: 353; on the symbolic status of the king's surplus body, see Slavoj Žižek, *The Sublime Object of Ideology* (London: Verso, 1989), 145–46, and Christopher Pye, *The Regal Phantasm: Shakespeare and the Politics of Spectacle* (London: Routledge, 1990), 1–8, 16–23, 168–72.

26 Slavoj Žižek, "Grimaces of the Real, or When the Phallus Appears," *October* 58, (fall 1991): 58. Žižek is speaking of the structure of phallic identification generally.

27 King James I, *Daemonologie*, 47; *A true and particular observation*, 257.

28 On the relation between witchcraft and aggression toward the maternal body, see Roper, *Oedipus and the Devil*, 210–18, and John Demos, *Entertaining Satan: Witchcraft and the Culture of Early New England* (Oxford: Oxford University Press, 1982), 116 ff, 179 ff.

29 Cotta, *Triall of Witch-craft*, 91, 92.

30 King James I, *Daemonologie*, 23. On "object small a" as a constitutive and inassimilable remainder—what is "in you more than you"—see Jacques Lacan, *Four Fundamental Concepts of Psychoanalysis*, ed. J.-A. Miller, trans. Alan Sheridan (New York: Norton, 1977), 174–86; Žižek, *Sublime Object*, 76–79; and Joan Copjec, "Vampires, Breast-Feeding, and Anxiety," *October* 58 (fall 1991): 31–35.

31 For a Lacanian reading of the uncanny "Thing" as a "kind of coagulated remnant of the liquid flux of *jouissance*" situated at the limit point of the symbolic, see Žižek, *The Sublime Object of Ideology*, 71. On the relation between the maternal and such a limit, and on the distinction between symbolic negation and the more rudimentary interdiction of the real that constitutes the symbolic register, see Copjec, "Vampires," esp. 29. On the "abjection" of the maternal as correlative to a specular, bolstering investment of the gap that founds signification, see Julia Kristeva, "Freud and Love: Treatment and its Discontents," in *The Kristeva Reader*, ed. Toril Moi (New York: Columbia University Press, 1986), 252–60; and Neil Hertz, *The End of the Line* (New York: Columbia University Press, 1985), 230–33. See also Lacan's often overlooked observation that the phallus is "negativity in its place in the *specular* image" (emphasis added) (*Ecrits*, 319).

32 Lacan, *Ecrits*, 315; Scot, *Discoverie of Witchcraft*, 282. On the insistence of the relation between the "object small a" and the specular image, see Žižek, "Grimaces," 55.

33 Scot, *Discoverie of Witchcraft*, 281, 12.

34 For a sixteenth-century reflection on the eye's inability to see itself, see Philip Barrough, *The Method of Physick* (London, 1590), 49; and Sergei Lobanov-Rostovsky, "Taming the Basilisk," in *The Body in Parts: Fantasies of Corporeality in Early Modern Europe*, ed. David Hillman and Carla Mazzio (New York: Routledge, 1997), 198.

35  Lacan, *Four Fundamental Concepts,* 82, 83. On the gaze as "object small a," especially in relation to the mediated spectatorial structures of Renaissance theater, see Barbara Freedman, *Staging the Gaze: Postmodernism, Psychoanalysis, and Shakespearean Comedy* (Ithaca, NY: Cornell University Press, 1991), 61–77.

36  On the relation between the gaze and the reflexive, Cartesian subject, see Lacan, *Four Fundamental Concepts,* 83. For historical claims for the significance of the Cartesian moment of mirroring self-reflection, see Richard Rorty, *Philosophy and the Mirror of Nature* (Princeton, NJ: Princeton University Press, 1979), 45–62; and Charles Taylor, *Sources of the Self: The Making of Modern Identity* (Cambridge, MA: Harvard University Press, 1989), 143–58.

37  Thomas Laqueur, *Making Sex: Body and Gender from the Greeks to Freud* (Cambridge, MA: Harvard University Press, 1990), 63–70, 88–113; and Greenblatt, *Shakespearean Negotiations,* 77–86.

38  On the anxiety attending the lack of the support of the lack, see Mladen Dolar, " 'I Shall Be with You on Your Wedding Night': Lacan and the Uncanny," *October* 58 (fall 1991): 13; and Eric Blumel, "*L'hallucination du double,*" *Analytica* 22 (1980): 49.

39  Laqueur, *Making Sex,* 74–75. On the association between theater and the scene of dissection, also see Michael Neill, *Issues of Death: Mortality and Identity in English Renaissance Tragedy* (Oxford: Oxford University Press, 1997), 102–40.

40  C. D. O'Malley, *Andreas Vesalius of Brussels, 1514–1564* (Berkeley: University of California, 1965), 143. Howard Marchitello associates the empty womb exposed with the gesture of turning the threat of nonmeaning back upon the woman ("Vesalius' *Fabrica* and Shakespeare's *Othello:* Anatomy, Gender, and the Narrative Production of Meaning," *Criticism* 35, no. 4 [fall 1993]: 544).

41  Patricia Parker, *Shakespeare from the Margins: Language, Culture, Context* (Chicago: University of Chicago Press, 1996), 234–39. Parker cites Helkiah Crooke, *Mikrocosmographia: A Description of the Body of Man* (London, 1618), 220.

42  Jonathan Sawday associates such images with a literal rendering of the injunction, "know thyself," as well as with an effort to naturalize the intrusive act of dissection: "The body willingly allowed the anatomist to assist the general process of decay" (*The Body Emblazoned: Dissection and the Human Body in Renaissance Culture* [London: Routledge, 1995], 112–17). See also, Neill, *Issues of Death,* 122–23.

43  Devon Hodges, *Renaissance Fictions of Anatomy* (Amherst: University of Massachusetts Press, 1985), 4–15.

44  Lacan, *Four Fundamental Concepts,* 85–90. On anamorphosis in relation to

misrecognition and the Renaissance spectatorial consciousness, see Freedman, *Staging the Gaze*, 27–35; on the relation between anamorphosis and the gaze in a political context, see Pye, *Regal Phantasm*, 89–95; on anamorphosis and the object a, see Ned Lukacher, "Anamorphic Stuff: Shakespeare, Catharsis, Lacan," *The South Atlantic Quarterly* 88 (fall 1989): 870–75; and Žižek, "Grimaces," 55–59.

45  Leo Steinberg, "The Line of Fate in Michelangelo's Painting," *Critical Inquiry* 6 (spring 1980): 431.

46  Leo Steinberg, *Michelangelo's Last Paintings* (New York: Oxford University Press, 1975), 40.

47  Julia Reinhard Lupton also sees St. Bartholomew's skin as an anamorphic form functioning within the genealogy of hagiography: "Whereas Bartholomew's skin is the metonymic attribute that identifies the saint, the iconicity extracted and displayed in his epidermal cloak serves as an attribute of hagiography as a genre, an anamorphic image that detaches from a phase of hagiography's formal structure and crystallizes it" (*Afterlives of the Saints: Hagiography, Typology, and Renaissance Literature* [Stanford: Stanford University Press, 1996], 48).

48  Charles de Tolnay, *Michelangelo* (Princeton: Princeton University Press, 1960), 5: 29.

49  Robert Clements, *Michelangelo's Theory of Art* (New York: New York University Press, 1961), 369–75.

50  William Heckscher, *Rembrandt's Anatomy of Dr. Nicolaas Tulp* (New York: New York University Press, 1958), 99.

51  Steinberg, *Last Paintings*, 62 fn.9. On Michelangelo's frequent reference in his poetry to his own dead skin, see Clements, *Michelangelo's Theory of Art*, 355–56.

52  Dante Alighieri, *The Inferno*, trans. John Sinclair (New York: Oxford University Press, 1974), 171–53. On Michelangelo's deep indebtedness to Dante generally, see de Tolnay, *Michelangelo*, and Clements, *Michelangelo's Theory of Art*. Michelangelo's contemporary, Benedetto Varchi, speaks of Dante's influence on *The Last Judgment* in particular; see Bernardine Barnes, *Michelangelo's* Last Judgment: *The Renaissance Response* (Berkeley: University of California Press, 1998), 97.

53  Leonard Barkan, *The Gods Made Flesh: Metamorphosis and the Pursuit of Paganism* (New Haven, CT: Yale University Press, 1986), 152. Barnes associates the skin with Marsyas, another familiar myth of punished overreaching (*Michelangelo's* Last Judgment, 106).

54  See Leonard Barkan, "Diana and Actaeon: The Myth as Synthesis," *English Literary Renaissance* 10 (1980): 322–28; and Pye, *Regal Phantasm*, 59–60.

55  Lacan, *Four Fundamental Concepts*, 89.

56 De Tolnay, *Michelangelo*, 5: 23. Although Barnes emphasizes the fresco's retention of older iconic and antiperspectival features in its construction of space (*Michelangelo's* Last Judgment, 37).

57 De Tolnay, *Michelangelo*, 5: 81.

58 *Ibid.*, 59, 128. In a superb analysis of the iconography of martyrdom, Julia Reinhard Lupton associates the saint's body generally, and Bartholomew's in particular, with just such a symbolic limit-point: "If the display of the saintly body represents the saint as image, as the proto-icon that prefigures all future iconography of the saints, this image [of the eviscerated body] partakes of the real insofar as it materializes the body as empty husk and pure surface without an underlying content. The skin of St. Bartholomew [as it is traditionally represented] is precisely such an empty sack or draped fabric, a sloughed hide and deflated container that could never be (re)embodied" (*Afterlives of the Saints*, 48).

59 Leo Steinberg, "A Corner of *The Last Judgment*," *Daedalus* 109 (spring 1980): 237.

60 Michel Foucault, "Prose of the World," in *The Order of Things: An Archaeology of the Human Sciences* (New York: Vintage, 1973). On the "hom(m)osexual," see Luce Irigaray, *This Sex Which Is Not One*, trans. Catherine Porter (Ithaca, NY: Cornell University Press, 1985), 170–91. For a critique of Irigaray's conflation of the homoerotic and the (patriarchal) male bond, see Eve Kosofsky Sedgwick, *Between Men: English Literature and Male Homosocial Desire* (New York: Columbia University Press, 1985), 19–20; and Jonathan Goldberg, *Sodometries: Renaissance Texts, Modern Sexualities* (Stanford: Stanford University Press, 1992), 276 n.16.

61 Lacan, *Four Fundamental Concepts*, 78.

62 Dolar, "Lacan and the Uncanny," 17.

63 Jürgen Habermas, *The Structural Transformation of the Public Sphere*, trans. Thomas Burger (Cambridge, MA: MIT Press), 54. On the significant early modern transition to an abstract, formal conception of law—the transition from law to The Law—in the English context, see Corrigan and Sayer, *The Great Arch*, 99–106.

64 Žižek, *Sublime Object of Ideology*, 80. See also Max Weber, "The Sociology of Charismatic Authority," in *From Max Weber: Essays in Sociology*, ed. H. H. Gerth and C. Wright Mills (New York: Oxford University Press, 1946).

65 Desiderius Erasmus, *Proverbes of Erasmus*, trans. Richard Taverner (London, 1545), fols. iiii–v.

66 For an account of a form of specular engagement that undoes the comforting ratio between proximity and distance, see William Flesch, "Proximity and Power: Shakespeare and Cinematic Space," *Theatre Journal* 39 (1987).

Although he is speaking in the context of theatricality and power, Flesch's work opens the possibility of a Blanchotian critique of some familiar versions of the historicist gaze.

## 3. Vanishing Point

1 The literature on the emergence of the vanishing point is considerable. See especially John White, *The Birth and Rebirth of Pictorial Space,* 3d edition (Cambridge, MA: Belknap, 1987); Samuel Edgerton Jr., *The Renaissance Discovery of Linear Perspective* (New York: Basic Books, 1975); Martin Jay, "Scopic Regimes of Modernity," in *Vision and Visuality,* ed. Hal Foster (Seattle: Bay, 1988); Hubert Damisch, *The Origin of Perspective,* trans. John Goodman (Cambridge, MA: MIT Press, 1995).

2 On the inverted message in the scene of Annunciation, see Erwin Panofsky, *Early Netherlandish Painting: Its Origins and Character* (Cambridge, MA: Harvard University Press, 153), 1: 138.

3 Georges Didi-Huberman, *Fra Angelico: Dissemblance and Figuration,* trans. Jane Marie Todd (Chicago: University of Chicago Press, 1995), 134.

4 Ibid., *Fra Angelico,* 115, 121.

5 Ibid., 128.

6 Michael Baxandall, *Painting and Experience in Fifteenth-Century Italy: A Primer in the Social History of Pictorial Style* (Oxford: Oxford University Press, 1974), 144.

7 Didi-Huberman, *Fra Angelico,* 149. On the spatial staging of conception in the Annunciation as a scene of aggressive erotic penetration, see Mary Ann Caws, *The Eye in the Text: Essays on Perception, Mannerist to Modern* (Princeton, NJ: Princeton University Press, 1981), 109–16.

8 Jacques Lacan, *Ecrits: A Selection,* trans. Alan Sheridan (New York: Norton, 1977), 302–8.

9 Christopher Pye, *The Regal Phantasm: Shakespeare and the Politics of Spectacle* (New York: Routledge, 1990), 29–42.

10 On the perspectivalism of the scene and its relation to the limits of a newly emerging illusionistic theater, see Jonathan Goldberg, "Perspectives: Dover Cliff and the Conditions of Representation," in *Shakespeare and Deconstruction,* ed. G. Douglas Atkins and David Bergeron (New York: Peter Lang, 1988), 245–65.

11 William Shakespeare, *King Lear,* in *The Arden Shakespeare,* ed. Kenneth Muir (London: Routledge, 1991). All subsequent references to *King Lear* will be to this edition and will be cited parenthetically in the text.

12 On the threat of annihilation and blindness implied by the scene, see Goldberg, "Perspectives," 251–56.

13 Goldberg observes that "the last objects seen are described in a kind of algebra that expresses a verbal version of a formula of proportion, a:b::b:c" (ibid., 250).

14 Jacques Lacan, *The Four Fundamental Concepts of Psychoanalysis*, ed. J.-A. Miller, trans. A. Sheridan (New York: Norton, 1981), 82.

15 Quoted in Muir, *The Arden Shakespeare*, 162. Stephen Greenblatt reads the play generally and the exorcism scene in particular as evidence of the play's selfconscious assertion of the distinction between theater and belief: "Demonic possession is responsibly marked out for the audience as a theatrical fraud, designed to gull the unsuspecting" (*Shakespearean Negotiations: The Circulation of Social Energy in Renaissance England* [Berkeley: University of California Press, 1988], 119). I am suggesting that the scene warns against the presumption that theatricality can be so comfortably equated with fraud and that theater's effects are so easily circumscribed.

16 Jean Laplanche and J.-B. Pontalis, eds., *The Language of Psychoanalysis*, trans. D. Nicholson-Smith (New York: Norton, 1973), 318.

17 On the recursive structure of fantasy, see Jean Laplanche and Jean-Bertrand Pontalis, "Fantasy and the Origins of Sexuality," in *Formations of Fantasy*, ed. Victor Burgin, James Donald, and Cora Kaplan (London: Methuen, 1986), 5-27.

18 On "inverted perspective," see Harold Osborne, ed., *The Oxford Companion to Art* (London: Oxford University Press, 1970), 846-57; on ecstasis and iconic representation, see Constantine Cavarnos, *Orthodox Iconography* (Belmont, MA: Institute for Byzantine and Modern Greek Studies, 1977), 43-44.

19 On the association between the image and devouring, incestuous desire, see Coppélia Kahn, "The Absent Mother in *King Lear*," in *Rewriting the Renaissance: The Discourse of Sexual Difference in Early Modern Europe*, ed. Margaret Ferguson, Maureen Quilligan, and Nancy Vickers (Chicago: University of Chicago Press, 1986), 41. On the connection between incest and Lear's "darker purpose," see Lynda Boose, "The Father and the Bride in Shakespeare," *PMLA* 97 (May 1982): 324-47.

20 Claude Lefort, *The Political Forms of Modern Society: Bureaucracy, Democracy, Totalitarianism*, ed. John Thompson (Cambridge, MA: MIT Press, 1986), 186-87.

21 Richard Halpern, *The Poetics of Primitive Accumulation: English Renaissance Culture and the Genealogy of Capital* (Ithaca, NY: Cornell University Press, 1991), 218.

22 For a reading of the scene as the return of the repressed maternal figure within Lear, see Janet Adelman, *Suffocating Mothers: Fantasies of Maternal Origin in Shakespeare's Plays*, Hamlet *to* The Tempest (New York: Routledge, 1992), 127-28; and Kahn, "The Absent Mother," 36.

23 Muir, *The Arden Shakespeare*, 205. Adelman notes the connection with the earlier evocation of the suffocating "mother" and associates it with the rising of Cordelia's heart within the king (*Suffocating Mothers*, 127).

24 Julia Kristeva, *Powers of Horror: An Essay on Abjection* (New York: Columbia University Press, 1982), 42.

25 Inasmuch as it amounts to the point where the relation between a founding transference or metaphorical positing and the metonymic signifying chain becomes undecidable, the return of the "mother" can be explicitly read as an undoing of or passing beyond fantasy, as well as the subjectivity associated with it.

26 On the significance of such a figure to early modernity, see Stephen Greenblatt, *Renaissance Self-Fashioning: From More to Shakespeare* (Chicago: The University of Chicago Press, 1980).

27 Jacqueline Rose, *States of Fantasy* (Oxford: Clarendon, 1996), 9.

28 Ibid.

29 On the image, see Pye, *The Regal Phantasm*, 73–81.

## 4. Dumb Hamlet

1 J. Dover Wilson, *What Happens in* Hamlet (Cambridge: Cambridge University Press, 1964), 2, 4, 23.

2 Terence Hawkes, "Telmah," in *Shakespeare and the Question of Theory*, ed. Patricia Parker and Geoffrey Hartman (New York: Methuen, 1985), 310–32.

3 These positions are held, respectively, by Wilson, *What Happens in* Hamlet, 174–98; Harvey Granville-Barker, *Prefaces to Shakespeare:* Hamlet (London: Sidgwick and Jackson, 1937), 90–97, and Andrew J. Green, "The Cunning of the Scene," *Shakespeare Quarterly* 4, no. 4 (October 1953) 395–404; W. W. Robson, "Did the King See the Dumb-Show?" *Cambridge Quarterly*, 6 (1972–75), 320–25; and L. C. Knights as cited in Robson, "Did the King See the Dumb-Show," 308–9.

4 All Shakespeare references in the chapter are to William Shakespeare, *Hamlet*, ed. Frank Kermode, in *The Riverside Shakespeare*, ed. G. Blakemore Evans et al. (Boston: Houghton Mifflin, 1974).

5 On the scene of ear poisoning as the "primal scene" of literature's subversion of speculative philosophy, see Ned Lukacher, *Primal Scenes: Literature, Philosophy, Psychoanalysis* (Ithaca, NY: Cornell University Press, 1986), 224–33. For Lukacher, the crux that opens limitless speculations about the origins of "The Murder of Gonzago" is a more general ambiguity concerning the king's presence: "The mystery of Claudius's whereabouts during the dumb show is the silent and almost undetectable trace that allows us to reconstruct Shakespeare's deconstruction of theatrical representation" (231). Otto Rank

reads the play within the play in terms of those elements of voyeurism, identification, and Oedipal aggression conventionally associated with the primal scene ("The Play within the Play in *Hamlet*," trans. Paul Lewison, *Journal of the Otto Rank Association* 6, no. 2 [December 1971]: 5–21).

6 On the general relation between the play-within-the-play scene, play, and transference neurosis, see Marjorie Garber, *Shakespeare's Ghost Writers: Literature as Uncanny Causality* (New York: Methuen, 1987), 160–61.

7 E. K. Chambers, *The Elizabethan Stage* (Oxford: Oxford University Press, 1923), 4: 227, 266–67, 280; William Rankins, *A Mirror of Monsters* (London, 1587); Edmund Grindal, Bishop of London, letter to Sir W. Cecil (Feb. 23, 1564); "Minutes of Privy Council" (May 13, 1580).

8 Anthony Munday, *A Second and Third Blast of Retrait from Plaies and Theaters* (1580; reprint, New York: Garland, 1973), 3.

9 Ibid., 2.

10 Stephen Gosson, *The School of Abuse* (London: Shakespeare Society, 1841), 44.

11 On the gaze in relation to the splitting of the subject, see Jacques Lacan, *The Four Fundamental Concepts of Psychoanalysis*, ed. J.-A. Miller, trans. A. Sheridan (New York: Norton, 1981), 67–78.

12 Wilson, *What Happens in* Hamlet, 3.

13 The experience of uncanny coalescence, of being at once caught out and called forth, can be intimate indeed. Tracing the path of controversy backward from Hawkes's "Telmah," to Wilson's *What Happens in* Hamlet, then to Wilson's first printed response to Greg's reading, I came at last to the ur-piece—W. W. Greg's 1917 article, "Hamlet's Hallucination." Greg opens his essay with some preliminary reflections on the status of ghosts during the era, before offering his "revolutionary" claim. "The full significance of this dumb-show has never been appreciated. Here and there a critic has dimly apprehended what it involved, but the vast majority have passed by with obstinate blindness." The decisive paragraph ends, however, with a footnote: "So far as I am aware, the only critic who clearly recognized the difficulty involved in the dumb-show was Pye. . . . But he did not pursue the matter" (W. W. Greg, "Hamlet's Hallucination," *Modern Language Review* 12, no. 4 [October 1917]: 397, 398). Enough to set the mind off balance? A frisson, for sure, from a thoroughly Hamlet-like experience of belatedness, but a frisson tempered by a not uncozy sense of belonging to a community of like minds extending all the way from Pye to Pye.

14 That the dumb show nevertheless does bear on such a regime is evident enough from the way it resonates beyond the Globe with another theatrical scene. "At these performances," Stephen Orgel writes of the court masque, "what the rest of the spectators watched was not a play but the queen at a play, and their response would have been not simply to the drama, but

to the relationship between the drama and its primary audience, the royal spectator" (*The Illusion of Power* [Berkeley: University of California Press, 1975], 9). And what the sovereign watched was herself—the narcissistic, often silent image of her own grandeur. The dumb show merely shows, to the extent that such power is irreducibly mediated, how easily narcissistic, absolutist power resolves into a scene structured around emptiness, like one of those anamorphic images in which the sovereign is suddenly seen to be a skull.

15  On the ghost as "the shape or sign of putting things in question," see Garber, *Shakespeare's Ghost Writers*, 164.

16  On sodomy and antitheatricalism, see Laura Levine, "Men in Women's Clothing: Anti-theatricality and Effeminization from 1579 to 1642," *Criticism* 28 (1986): 121–43; and Stephen Orgel, "Nobody's Perfect: Or, Why Did the English Stage Take Boys for Women?" in *Displacing Homophobia,* ed. Ronald Butters, John Clum, and Michael Moon (Durham, NC: Duke University Press, 1989), 7–29. On the "invention" of homosexuality— its passage from a category of act to a "species"—see Michel Foucault, *The History of Sexuality, Volume I, An Introduction,* trans. Robert Hurley (New York: Pantheon, 1978), 43; and Alan Bray, *Homosexuality in Renaissance England* (London: Gay Men's Press, 1982). On the relationship between homoerotic collaboration and the changing conception of authorship during the seventeenth century, see Jeffrey Masten, *Textual Intercourse: Collaboration, Authorship, and Sexualities in Renaissance Drama* (Cambridge: Cambridge University Press, 1997). For an important analysis of sodomy as the category of categorical confusion per se—an epistemological and ontological limit—during the Renaissance, as well as a subtle account of the complex points of intersection between early modern and modern regimes of sexuality, see Jonathan Goldberg, *Sodometries: Renaissance Texts, Modern Sexualities* (Stanford: Stanford University Press, 1992), esp. 18–25, 121–25.

17  When railing against the powers of the stage, the antitheatricalist may have in mind orifices other than that which one might at first imagine. Why does one guard against the frontal assault of evil with our moral injunctions, Gosson asks, while allowing it through theater "in the posterior" (*School of Abuse,* 32)?

18  Francis Barker, *The Tremulous Private Body: Essays on Subjection* (London: New York: Methuen, 1984), 1–53; Terry Eagleton, *William Shakespeare* (Oxford: Blackwell, 1986), 70–75.

19  On the connection between Pyrrhus's and Hamlet's hesitation, see Harry Levin, *The Question of* Hamlet (New York: Viking, 1959), 151; and James L. Calderwood, *To Be and Not To Be: Negation and Metadrama in* Hamlet (New York: Columbia University Press, 1983), 147.

20  On the relation between such a "mimetic crisis" and the potentially limitless cycles of revenge, see René Girard: "Hamlet's Dull Revenge," in *Literary Theory/Renaissance Texts*, ed. Patricia Parker and David Quint (Baltimore, MD: Johns Hopkins University Press, 1986), 282–90; " 'To Entrap the Wisest': A Reading of *The Merchant of Venice*," in *Literature and Society: Selected Papers from the English Institute*, ed. Edward Said (Baltimore, MD: Johns Hopkins University Press, 1980), 104–7; and *Violence and the Sacred*, trans. Patrick Gregory (Baltimore, MD: Johns Hopkins University Press, 1972), 39–67.

21  On Hamlet's oedipal identification and its relation to delay, see Ernest Jones, *Hamlet and Oedipus* (New York: Norton, 1949), 99–100. On Pyrrhus problematically condensing the figures of Hamlet and Claudius, see David Scott Kastan, " 'His semblable is his mirror': Hamlet and the Imitation of Revenge," *Shakespeare Studies* 19 (1981): 113; and Clifford Leech, "The Hesitation of Pyrrhus," in *The Morality of Art: Essays Presented to G. Wilson Knight*, ed. D. W. Jefferson (New York: Barnes and Noble, 1969), 46.

22  Wilson, "What Happens in Hamlet," 266–67. On the consensus over the transforming effects of the voyage, see Calderwood, *To Be and Not To Be*, 34; and Susan Snyder, *The Comic Matrix of Shakespeare's Tragedies* (Princeton, NJ: Princeton University Press, 1979), 123. Hamlet's change "takes place in that great off-stage void from which only ghosts, ambassadors, and pirate messengers return," Calderwood remarks (*To Be and Not To Be*, 37).

23  Jacques Lacan, *Ecrits: A Selection*, trans. A. Sheridan (New York: Norton, 1977), 314–27. That such a remainder lies at the opaque heart of the play is suggested by A. W. Schlegel's observation: "This enigmatical work resembles those irrational equations in which a fraction of unknown magnitude always remains, that will in no way admit of solution" (*A Course of Lectures on Dramatic Art and Literature*, trans. John Black [London: Bell and Daldy, 1871], 404).

24  On specular rivalry and identification—the familiar components of the "mirror stage"—in Hamlet's relationship to Laertes at the close of the play, see Jacques Lacan, "Desire and the Interpretation of Desire in *Hamlet*," in *Literature and Psychoanalysis: The Question of Reading, Otherwise*, ed. Shoshana Felman (New Haven, CT: Yale French Studies, 1977), 31.

25  On the structure of the homosocial bond, see Eve Kosofsky Sedgwick, *Between Men: English Literature and Male Homosocial Desire* (New York: Columbia University Press, 1985). For some brief, suggestive remarks on homosociality in *Hamlet*, see Jonathan Crewe, *Trials of Authorship: Anterior Forms and Poetic Reconstruction from Wyatt to Shakespeare* (Berkeley: University of California Press, 1990), 77.

26  On Hamlet's new resignation after the sea voyage, as well as a newfound

ability to "admire unpremeditated action," see Calderwood, *To Be and Not To Be*, 34. On his "new calmness" and submission to a "pattern he may perceive but did not create," see Snyder, *The Comic Matrix*, 123.

27 On representing Claudius in the wager, see Lacan, "Desire and the Interpretation of Desire in *Hamlet*," 29. On the fictional nature of the world of the duel, see Calderwood, *To Be and Not To Be*, 45; and Lacan, "Desire and the Interpretation of Desire in *Hamlet*," 32.

28 Lacan, "Desire and the Interpretation of Desire in *Hamlet*," 33–34. On the insistence of negation and its positive verbal effects in *Hamlet*, see Calderwood, *To Be and Not To Be*, 53–58.

29 "Hamlet is constantly suspended at the time of the Other, throughout the entire story until the very end" (Lacan, "Desire and the Interpretation of Desire in *Hamlet*," 17).

30 On the historical relation between the emergence of the pictorial vanishing point and the transcendent subject, see Norman Bryson, *Vision and Painting: The Logic of the Gaze* (New Haven, CT: Yale University Press, 1983), 87–131; and Brian Rotman, *Signifying Nothing: The Semiotics of Nothing* (New York: St. Martin's, 1987).

31 It is not surprising that the effeminate courtier should also be the object of economic demonization. As Luce Irigaray has argued, homosocial structuring is congruent with the heightened emergence of capitalist relations, for the very distinction between producer and commodity is maintained through the intensification of the specular, exclusionary bonds that inscribe the woman in the position of third term, the necessary and purely negative term of exchange, that is, the phallus (*This Sex Which Is Not One*, trans. Catherine Porter [Ithaca, NY: Cornell University Press, 1985], 170–91). On the association of the woman and the phallus in structures of exchange, see also Lacan, *Ecrits*, 207.

32 Patricia Parker describes Fortinbras's arrival at the end of the play as "something like the beginnings of the modern state" (*Shakespeare at the Margins*, 257).

33 My account of the transference of Hamlet's dying voice and the political contradictions that attend it is consonant with Francis Barker's claim that Fortinbras's arbitrary military intervention figures the larger compromise through which the play resolves its inability to conceive its historicity except in terms of a discourse of sovereignty, which it at once takes to be absolute and acknowledges to be residual ("Which Dead? Hamlet and the Ends of History," in *Uses of History: Marxism, Postmodernism, and the Renaissance*, ed. Francis Barker, Peter Hulme, and Margaret Iverson [Manchester: Manchester University Press, 1991], 53–54).

34 Calderwood associates the act with Hamlet's problematic identification with a multitude of fathers and kings (*To Be and Not To Be*, 96).

35  Richard Halpern, *The Poetics of Primitive Accumulation: English Renaissance Culture and the Genealogy of Capital* (Ithaca, NY: Cornell University Press, 1991), 44–49. On the general connection between the play and the emerging machinery of state, see Parker, *Shakespeare at the Margins*, 260.

36  "Of course this refers to the King, as Warburton long ago pointed out. But strange to say, Theobald referred it to Hamlet, a noteworthy slip in one of the best editors Shakespeare ever had, and it is quite as remarkable that the slip escaped the notice of the subsequent Variorum editors, who omitted no chance of making merry over 'poor Tib and his Toxophilus'" (Horace H. Furness, ed., *A New Variorum Edition of Shakespeare*, vol. 3 [Philadelphia: Lippincott, 1877], 456).

37  On *capitonage*, see Jacques Lacan, "The Subversion of the Subject in the Dialectic of Desire," in *Ecrits*, 292–324; and Slavoj Žižek, *The Sublime Object of Ideology* (London: Verso, 1989), 87–105.

38  Julia Kristeva, "Freud and Love: Treatment and Its Discontents," in *The Kristeva Reader*, ed. Toril Moi (New York: Columbia University Press, 1986), 242. Julia Lupton and Kenneth Reinhard read the specularity of the "Willow Song" as suggestive of the reflective relation between Ophelia and Gertrude, a convergence that threatens a convergence between the object of desire and the "undialectized" Other (*After Oedipus: Shakespeare in Psychoanalysis* [Ithaca, NY: Cornell University Press, 1993], 81–82).

39  Lacan, "Desire and the Interpretation of Desire," 23. Glossing Lacan, Lupton and Reinhard claim that through her death "Ophelia is 'reintegrated' as an object in desire" (*After Oedipus*, 77).

40  On the relation between the ghost and uncanny recurrence, see Garber, *Shakespeare's Ghost Writers*, 127–32, 172–76. On its relation to transference in the context of the psychoanalytic session, see Julia Lupton and Kenneth Reinhard, "Shapes of Grief: Freud, *Hamlet*, and Mourning," *Genders* 4 (March 1989): 60.

41  Kristeva, "Freud and Love," 241–44, 253. Consider in this context Hamlet's claim that the First Player's speech is drawn from a play "well digested in the scenes," in which others have tasted "no sallets in the lines to make the matter savory" (2.2.439–42). On Freud's suppression of the pre-oedipal dynamic of introjection and mourning in the play, see Lupton and Reinhard, "Shapes of Grief," 57–8. Garber associates Hamlet's act of remembrance with ingestion (*Shakespeare's Ghost Writers*, 150).

42  Žižek, *Sublime Object of Ideology*, 180. For Lacan's account of *l'extimité*, see *Four Fundamental Concepts*, 363. On *das Ding* and its relations to the pleasure principle, the paternal law, and the mechanisms of symbolic interpellation, see Jacques Lacan, *The Seminar of Jacques Lacan: Book VII: The Ethics of Psychoanalysis, 1959–1960*, ed. J.-A. Miller, trans. Dennis Porter (New York: Norton, 1992), 43–138, esp. 56.

43   Žižek, *Sublime Object of Ideology*, 71, 180.

44   Jürgen Habermas, *The Structural Transformation of the Public Sphere: An Inquiry into a Category of Bourgeois Society*, trans. Thomas Burger (Cambridge, MA: MIT Press, 1991), 28, 54.

45   On the radical "disincorporation" of the individual attending the undoing of the body politic and the disengagement of a civil society from the state, see Claude Lefort, *The Political Forms of Modern Society: Bureaucracy, Democracy, Totalitarianism*, ed. John Thompson (Cambridge, MA: MIT Press, 1986), 297–306.

46   On the anal-erotic associations of the ear-poisoning scene, see Ernest Jones, "The Death of Hamlet's Father," *International Journal of Psychoanalysis*, 29 (1948): 174–76. On the obscene, anal "Father of Enjoyment," see Slavoj Žižek, *Looking Awry: An Introduction to Jacques Lacan through Popular Culture* (Cambridge, MA: MIT Press, 1991), 24, and "Grimaces of the Real, or When the Phallus Appears," *October* 58 (fall 1991): 56.

47   On the same-sex theory, see Thomas Laqueur, *Making Sex: Body and Gender from the Greeks to Freud* (Cambridge, MA: Harvard University Press, 1990), 63–70, 88–113; and Stephen Greenblatt, *Shakespearean Negotiations: The Circulation of Social Energy in Renaissance England* (Berkeley: University of California Press, 1988), 77–86.

48   On the relation between revenge, reenactment, and mimetic theory, see David Scott Kastan, " 'His semblable is his mirror': Hamlet and the Imitation of Revenge," *Shakespeare Studies* 19 (1981): 111–22. On the dumb show as a stylized counter to "theater as the space of good imitation," see Lukacher, *Primal Scenes*, 229. On its hearkening back to an archaic nonillusionistic form of representation derived from the Morality tradition, see Howard Felperin, *Shakespearean Representation: Mimesis and Modernity in Elizabethan Tragedy* (Princeton, NJ: Princeton University Press, 1977), 46–48. Lupton and Reinhard associate the selfconscious archaism of *Hamlet*'s Senecan set-pieces with a structure of pre-oedipal mourning through which the play itself incorporates a form that it nevertheless designates as prior and alien to it, the equivalent, at the level of literary form, of the structures of incorporation traced in the scene of ear poisoning (*After Oedipus*, 103–4).

49   Cynthia Chase, "The Witty Butcher's Wife: Freud, Lacan, and the Conversion of the Resistance to Theory," *Modern Language Notes* 102, no. 5 (December 1987): 1010.

50   For a subtle account of the mythology of England's descent from fallen Troy, see Jeffrey Knapp, *An Empire Nowhere: England, America, and Literature from* Utopia *to* The Tempest (Berkeley: University of California Press, 1992), 41–49. Elizabeth Bellamy persuasively argues that Troy amounts to the primal repressed of epic history, its unrepresentable and recurrent ground, and thus the repressed that founds the unconscious subject within

epic's imperial and dynastic order; as primal repressed, Troy only ever appears in the form of its vanishing (*Translations of Power: Narcissism and the Unconscious in Epic History* [Ithaca, NY: Cornell University Press, 1993], 34–37, 54–81). *Hamlet* suggests that falling Ilium figures a more radical horizon, not the return of the repressed from within epic narrative but the limit of symbolization as such, and thus the point at which every narratable history falters. The subjectivity emerging at that vanishing point is defined not by narcissistic affirmation but by a curiously fixating ekphrasis—consider Aeneas "fastened in a stare, astonished" (stupet obtutuque haeret defixus in uno) by the murals of Ilium's fall, or Lucrece spurring her own deadly despair with "Troy's painted woes": "She lends them words, and she their looks doth borrow" (Virgil, *The Aeneid*, in *Virgili Maronis Opera*, ed. F. A. Hirtzel [1890; reprint, Oxford: Oxford University Press, 1966], 1.1.495; William Shakespeare, *The Rape of Lucrece*, ed. Hallett Smith, in *Riverside Shakespeare*, 1.1498). The grounds of that transferential fixation are suggested by Queen Margaret's account of the seductive powers of an Ascanius-like go-between in Henry VI, part 2:

> "How often have I tempted Suffolk's tongue . . .
> To sit and witch me, as Ascanius did
> When he to madding Dido would unfold
> His father's acts commenc'd in burning Troy! (3.2.116–19)

Sexuality, dynastic history, and mythic origination are articulated around the seductive potency of the mediator and go-between, around the bewitchments of language itself. But if there is madness here, it is precisely in the prospect that the mediating function of language might fail in the strange catachresis of the sitting tongue, symbolization's fascinating, disastrous convergence with *das Ding*. The association between Troy, ekphrasis, and incorporation is apparent in the description of Aeneas's absorption: "He feeds his soul on what is nothing but a picture" (animum pictura pascit inani) 1.1.464. It is also evident in the painted image of Nestor from *The Rape of Lucrece*:

> There pleading might you see grave Nestor stand,
>
> . . . . . . . . . . . . . . . . . . . . .
>
> In speech it seem'd his beard, all silver white,
> Wagg'd up and down, and from his lips did fly
> Thin winding breath, which purl'd up to the sky.
> About him were a press of gaping faces,
> Which seem'd to swallow up his sound advice. (ll.1401–1409)

On the relation between ekphrasis and unconscious affect, see Bellamy, *Translations of Power*, 60–69.

51 T. S. Eliot, "Hamlet and His Problems," in *The Sacred Wood* (London: Methuen, 1960), 101.

52 Wilson, *What Happens in* Hamlet, 7.


## 5. Subject Matter

1 All quotes in epigraph from William Shakespeare, *Hamlet*, ed. Frank Kermode, in *The Riverside Shakespeare*, ed. G. Blakemore Evans (Boston: Houghton Mifflin, 1974). Subsequent references to the play will be from this edition and will be cited in the text by act, scene and line number only.

2 That is, I focus on matter understood in and beyond its limited manifestation in the subject/object doublet, matter as the thing rather than the object. At the same time, though my account of matter will at times coincide with *das Ding* as it is described within the Lacanian framework, I avoid reference to that technical term in this context in order to stay as closely attuned as possible to early modern usage.

3 Lorrain Daston, "Marvelous Facts and Miraculous Evidence in Early Modern Europe," *Critical Inquiry* 18 (1991): 93–113. See also by Daston: "The Factual Sensibility," *Isis* 79, no. 298 (1988): 452–67; "Baconian Facts and the Prehistory of Objectivity," in *Rethinking Objectivity*, ed. Allan Megill (Durham, NC: Duke University Press, 1994), 42–47; and, with Katherine Park, *Wonders and the Order of Nature: 1150–1750* (New York: Zone Books, 1998), 215–36. On the postmedieval breakdown of "universalism" and the ascendancy of "particularism," see Stephen Greenblatt, "Meaning and Mutilation," in *The Body in Parts: Fantasies of Corporeality in Early Modern Europe*, ed. David Hillman and Carla Mazzio (New York: Routledge, 1997), 229.

4 Joy Kenseth, " 'A World of Wonders in One Closet Shut,' " in *The Age of the Marvelous*, ed. Joy Kenseth (Hanover, NH: Hood Museum of Art-Dartmouth College, 1991), 83–84; Krzysztof Pomian, *Collectors and Curiosities: Paris and Venice, 1500–1800*, trans. Elizabeth Wiles-Portier (Cambridge: Polity, 1990), 45–50; Paula Findlen, "Jokes of Nature and Jokes of Knowledge: The Playfulness of Scientific Discourse in Early Modern Europe," *Renaissance Quarterly* 43 (summer 1990): 311; Michel Foucault, *The Order of Things: An Archaeology of the Human Sciences* (New York: Vintage, 1973), 17–45.

5 Cited in Jonathan Sawday, *The Body Emblazoned: Dissection and the Human Body in Renaissance Culture* (London: Routledge, 1995), 233.

6 Daston, "The Factual Sensibility," 466. Steven Mullaney also emphasizes the relative autonomy allowed the object in such collections, albeit ultimately in the service of cultural appropriation (*The Place of the Stage: License,*

*Play, and Power in Renaissance England* [Chicago: University of Chicago Press, 1988], 62).

7 For a parallel instance of the things—in this case, skeletons—of the cabinet spilling over into the adjoining library, see William Schupbach, "Collections of Curiosities in Academic Institutions," in *The Origins of Museums: The Cabinets of Curiosities in Sixteenth and Seventeenth-Century Europe*, ed. Oliver Impey and Arthur MacGregor (Oxford: Clarendon, 1985), 172.

8 Giuseppe Olmi, "Science-Honour-Metaphor: Italian Cabinets of the Sixteenth and Seventeenth Centuries," in *The Origins of Museums*, 9–10.

9 Amy Boesky, "'Outlandish-Fruits': Commissioning Nature for the Museum of Man," *English Literary History* 58 (1991): 322.

10 Pomian, *Collectors and Curiosities*, 56–57.

11 Barbara Maria Stafford speaks of "Rarities" being "conjured into life by the activity of looking" (*Artful Science: Enlightenment, Entertainment, and the Eclipse of Visual Education* [Cambridge, MA: MIT Press, 1994], 221).

12 William Pietz, "The Problem of the Fetish, I," *Res* 9 (spring 1985), 5–17.

13 On the prevalence in these collections of the recently acquired artifacts of "primitive" cultures, see Mullaney, *Place of the Stage*, 60–75; and Anthony Alan Shelton, "Cabinets of Transgression: Renaissance Collections and the Incorporation of the New World," in *The Cultures of Collecting*, ed. John Elsner and Roger Cardinal (London: Reaktion, 1994), 176–201.

14 Jacques Lacan, *Ecrits: A Selection*, trans. Alan Sheridan (New York: Norton, 1977), 166–67.

15 Pomian, *Collectors and Curiosities*, 70–76.

16 Note in this context the presence of Caravaggio's Medusa among the "unicorn horns," Native American parrot feather cloaks, and the "exceptionally strong magnet" of the Medici cabinet in Florence, as well as the anamorphic portraits of Henry IV and Louis XIII in Tradescant's cabinet (Kenseth, "A World of Wonders," 82, 88). On the association between the Medusa's head and the emphasis on natural metamorphosis in the collections, see Findlen, "Jokes of Nature," 311.

17 Pomian, *Collectors and Curiosities*, 77, 103. The threat of absorption may also be suggested by the persistence with which images of the collections include the figure of the "pointer" or guide within the scene of wonders, a recourse that of course troubles the very boundary it may intend to secure. Consider also the inscription on the Cerutti wonder cabinet: "Viewer, insert your eyes" (cited in Daston and Park, *Wonders*, 153). The relation between fetishism and the gaze runs deep, judging from Freud's exemplary instance of fetishism, the case of the Wolf Man, whose erotic obsession with a particular "shine on the nose" Freud was able to translate, by way of a phonemic equivalence between the man's native Russian and his childhood En-

glish, into a "glance at the nose," a glance which in turn stands in for and against the dreaded sight of lack ("Fetishism," in *The Standard Edition of the Complete Psychological Works of Sigmund Freud*, ed. James Strachey (London: Hogarth, 1961), 21: 152–57). To conclude from this that the fetishistic subject latches onto a simulacrum that stands in the place of the missing part—the familiar account of the fetish—does not capture what is exemplary about the example, that is, the way the act of looking is crystallized in the object seen, a shine equated with a glance. In that conflation, one can recognize the ultimate grounds for the fetish's captivating properties, as well as the entire economy of repudiation and renewed loss it embodies. Not simply a reassuring compromise object in place of a loss, the fetish actively plays out and shores against that originating split in the experience of being inscribed within—"fascinated" by—the gaze as it derives from elsewhere.

18 Barbara Maria Stafford remarks apropos the wonder cabinet that "browsing nature for possible possessions was akin to shopping" (*Artful Science*, 218). On the transition from a "metaphysical" to a "mercantile"—"man-centered, pragmatic"—world, see Shelton, "Cabinets of Transgression," 201. On the relation between the curiosity and the advent of the (bourgeois) public sphere, see Daston and Park, *Wonders*, 218.

19 On the animating surfaces of the Dutch still-life, see Hal Foster, "The Art of Fetishism: Notes on Dutch Still Life," in *Fetishism as Cultural Discourse*, ed. Emily Apter and William Pietz (Ithaca, NY: Cornell University Press, 1993), 254–55.

20 On mourning and incorporation, see Sigmund Freud, "Mourning and Melancholia," in *The Standard Edition of the Complete Psychological Works of Sigmund Freud*, ed. James Strachey, vol. 14 (London: Hogarth, 1961).

21 Jacques Lacan, "Desire and the Interpretation of Desire in *Hamlet*," in *Literature and Psychoanalysis: The Question of Reading, Otherwise*, ed. Shoshana Felman (New Haven, CT: Yale French Studies, 1977): 38.

22 On the significant emergence during the Renaissance of an incorporative, not just reflective, relation between micro- and macrocosm, see Frances Yates, *The Art of Memory* (Harmondsworth, England: Penguin, 1969), 152.

23 On the historical relation between museums and tombs, see Hubert Damisch, "The Museum Device: Notes on Institutional Changes," *Lotus International* 35 (1982): 5. On mourning and incorporation, see Julia Lupton and Kenneth Reinhard, *After Oedipus: Shakespeare in Psychoanalysis* (Ithaca, NY: Cornell University Press, 1993), 114, 120, 139. On encryption, see Nicolas Abraham and Maria Torok, *The Wolf Man's Magic Word: A Cryptonymy*, trans. Nicholas Rand (Minneapolis: University of Minnesota Press, 1986).

24 On "inner talismans," see Yates, *Art of Memory*, 118, 157. On the association between the curiosity cabinet and the memory theater, see Olmi, "Science-Honour-Metaphor," 7; and Adalgisa Lugli, *Naturalia et Mirabilia. Il col-*

*lezionismo enciclopedico nelle Wunderkammern d'Europa* (Milan: Mazzotta, 1990), 79 ff.

25 Michael Neill, *Issues of Death: Mortality and Identity in English Renaissance Tragedy* (Oxford: Oxford University Press, 1997), 139.

26 The association between a lurid scene of revenge enacted and the cool world of Baconian facts becomes less improbable if one keeps in mind that the term *fact* derives from *act*, particularly a criminal act, a derivation preserved in the legal usage, "after the fact." See Daston, "Baconian Facts," 45.

27 James Calderwood, *To Be and Not To Be* (New York: Columbia University Press, 1983), 60, 89.

28 Jean Laplanche and J.-B. Pontalis, eds., *The Language of Psychoanalysis*, trans. D. Nicholson-Smith (New York: Norton, 1973), 318.

29 On the association between "mother" and "matter" in the scene, see Margaret Ferguson, 'Hamlet: Letters and Spirits," in *Shakespeare and the Question of Theory*, ed. Patricia Parker and Geoffrey Hartman (New York: Methuen, 1985), 295; Parker, *Shakespeare at the Margins*, 254, 262; Avi Erlich, *Hamlet's Absent Father* (Princeton, NJ: Princeton University Press, 1977), 214–18.

30 William Shakespeare, *Hamlet*, vol. 2, ed. Horace Furness, in Furness, ed., *A New Variorum Edition of Shakespeare*, 29 vols. (Philadelphia: Lippincott, 1879), 4: 98.

31 The "mobled queen" is not so much a reflexive reference to such a mute limit as it is an index of the arbitrary force necessary to posit language in that self-referential form. See Paul de Man, "Hypogram and Inscription: Michael Riffaterre's Poetics of Reading," in *The Resistance to Theory* (Minneapolis: University of Minnesota Press, 1986). I am indebted to Scott McMillin for first drawing my attention to the importance of the figure of Hecuba in the play, a figure he reads as suggestive of the fundamental relation between maternal abjection and the practice of acting ("Shakespeare's Troy: The Space of Narcissism and Theatre" and "Can Hamlet be Cured," unpublished manuscripts).

32 The ambiguity of the corpse is at a certain level already present in the fetish. Freud remains undecided whether the distinctive form of knowledge that characterizes the fetishist—a simultaneous knowing and not knowing—is a matter of *Verdrangung*, the repression and negation that constitutes the subject within the chain of signification, or of *Verleugnung*, the more radical disavowal of that structuring lack. That situating of the fetish at once in and beyond castration, in and beyond symbolization, becomes apparent at the point in Freud's account where fetishism becomes indistinguishable from mourning. In the fetish, Freud says, "the horror of castration has set up a memorial to itself," as if the horror of castration were at the same time a horror lest such a horror be lost, as if it were the loss of loss that the fetish

shored against ("Fetishism," 153, 154). Ferguson also takes the scene of Polonius's death to be pivotal, seeing in his "incorpsing" the murderously definitive splitting of matter and spirit in the play and a corresponding reduction of ethical possibilities for the hero and formal possibilities for the drama ("Letters and Spirits," 298–99).

33  In that regard, one should attend less to the scandalous fact of the King's nothingness—an oedipal recognition—than to the hesitation that makes even that recognition a stopgap and an alibi: "The King is a thing . . . / 'A thing,' my Lord? / Of nothing." "This nothing's more than matter," Laertes says elsewhere (4.5.174). Neither a thing nor, exactly, nothing: understood in relation to that wavering, political and symbolic disincorporation means the insistence of a phantasmatic thingness of the social body as much as it means its emptiness.

34  Richard Halpern, *The Poetics of Primitive Accumulation: English Renaissance Culture and the Genealogy of Capital* (Ithaca, NY: Cornell University Press, 1991), 74.

35  Karl Marx, *Capital: A Critique of Political Economy*, trans. Ben Fowkes (New York: Vintage, 1977), 1: 128, 138.

36  Thomas Keenan, "The Point is to (Ex)Change It," in *Fetishism as Cultural Discourse*, 169.

37  Amy Boesky, " 'Outlandish-Fruits,' " 318. On the connection between the wonder cabinet and the Renaissance anatomy theater, see Neill, *Issues of Death*, 117.

38  "From the mid-sixteenth century, [the anatomy theater's] quasi-commercial character was emphasized by the growing practice of selling tickets to the large audiences attracted through public advertisement; and their consciously theatrical effect was enhanced by the erection, in many parts of Europe, of increasingly lavish, purpose-built amphitheatres, where two or three hundred spectators could watch the brilliantly illuminated spectacle, which typically lasted for up to five days" (Neill, *Issues of Death*, 115).

39  On the allegorical dimensions of the scene in relation to the staging of the anatomist's authority, see Jonathan Sawday, *The Body Emblazoned*, 72–74.

40  Claude Lefort, *The Political Forms of Modern Society: Bureaucracy, Democracy, Totalitarianism*, ed. John Thompson (Cambridge, MA: MIT Press, 1986), 305.

41  Walter Benjamin, *The Origin of German Tragic Drama*, trans. John Osborne (London: New Left Books, 1977), 140, 192.

42  For suggestive reflections on the paradoxical relation between the bourgeois *bouleversement* of social relations and the production of historicism's recuperative "phantom of continuous creation," see Damisch, "The Museum Device," 9–10.

43 William Shakespeare, *Julius Caesar,* ed. Frank Kermode, in *The Riverside Shakespeare,* 2.1.63–65.
44 One might recall, in this context, that in his dramatic career Polonius had played Julius Caesar: "It was a brute part of him to kill so capital a calf" (3.2.104). Ferguson remarks on the connection with Polonius's sacrificial function in the play ("Letters and Spirits," 298).

# Works Cited

Abraham, Nicolas and Maria Torok. *The Wolf Man's Magic Word: A Crypto-nymy.* Trans. Nicholas Rand. Minneapolis: University of Minnesota Press, 1986.

Adelman, Janet. *Suffocating Mothers: Fantasies of Maternal Origin in Shake-speare's Plays,* Hamlet *to* The Tempest. New York: Routledge, 1992.

Agnew, Jean-Christophe. *Worlds Apart: The Market and the Theater in Anglo-American Thought, 1550–1750.* Cambridge: Cambridge University Press, 1986.

Ankarloo, Bengt, and Gustav Henningsen, eds. *Early Modern European Witchcraft: Centres and Peripheries.* Oxford: Clarendon, 1993.

Apter, Emily, and William Pietz, eds. *Fetishism as Cultural Discourse.* Ithaca, NY: Cornell University Press, 1993.

Bacon, Francis. *Novum Organum.* In *The Works of Francis Bacon,* ed. Basil Montagu. 17 vols. (London: 1620).

Barkan, Leonard. *The Gods Made Flesh: Metamorphosis and the Pursuit of Paganism.* New Haven, CT: Yale University Press, 1986.

———. "Diana and Actaeon: The Myth as Synthesis." *English Literary Renaissance* 10 (1980): 322–28.

Barker, Francis. *The Tremulous Private Body: Essays on Subjection.* London: Methuen, 1984.

———. "Which Dead? Hamlet and the Ends of History." In *Uses of History: Marxism, Postmodernism, and the Renaissance,* ed. Francis Barker, Peter Hulme, and Margaret Iverson. Manchester: Manchester University Press, 1991.

Barnes, Bernardine. *Michelangelo's* Last Judgment: *The Renaissance Response.* Berkeley: University of California Press, 1998.

Barrough, Philip. *The Method of Physick.* London, 1590.

Bartisan, Georges. *Opthalmologeia.* Dresden, 1583.

Baxandall, Michael. *Painting and Experience in Fifteenth-Century Italy: A Primer in the Social History of Pictorial Style.* Oxford: Oxford University Press, 1974.

Bellamy, Elizabeth J. *Translations of Power: Narcissism and the Unconscious in Epic History.* Ithaca, NY: Cornell University Press, 1993.

Belsey, Catherine. *The Subject of Tragedy: Identity and Difference in Renaissance Drama.* London: Methuen, 1985.

Benjamin, Walter. *The Origin of German Tragic Drama.* Trans. John Osborne. London: New Left Books, 1977.

# Works Cited

Bhabha, Homi K. "DissemiNation." In *Nation and Narration,* ed. Homi K. Bhabha. New York: Routledge, 1990.

Blumel, Eric. "*L'hallucination du double.*" *Analytica* 22 (1980): 124–36.

Boesky, Amy. " 'Outlandish-Fruits': Commissioning Nature for the Museum of Man." *English Literary History* 58 (1991): 305–30.

Boose, Lynda. "The Father and the Bride in Shakespeare." *PMLA* 97 (May 1982): 324–47.

Bray, Alan. *Homosexuality in Renaissance England.* London: Gay Men's Press, 1982.

Briggs, Robin. " 'Many reasons why': Witchcraft and the Problem of Multiple Explanation." In *Witchcraft in Early Modern Europe,* ed. Jonathan Barry, Marianne Hester, and Gareth Roberts. Cambridge: Cambridge University Press, 1996.

Bryson, Norman. *Vision and Painting: The Logic of the Gaze.* New Haven, CT: Yale University Press, 1983.

Calderwood, James L. *To Be and Not To Be: Negation and Metadrama in Hamlet.* New York: Columbia University Press, 1983.

Cavarnos, Constantine. *Orthodox Iconography.* Belmont, MA: Institute for Byzantine and Modern Greek Studies, 1977.

Caws, Mary Ann. *The Eye in the Text: Essays on Perception, Mannerist to Modern.* Princeton, NJ: Princeton University Press, 1981.

Ceruti, B. and A. Chiocco. *Musaeum Francisci Calceolari Veronensis.* Verona, 1622.

Chambers, E. K. *The Elizabethan Stage.* Vol. 4. Oxford: Oxford University Press, 1923.

Charnes, Linda. *Notorious Identity: Materializing the Subject in Shakespeare.* Cambridge, MA: Harvard University Press, 1993.

Chase, Cynthia. "The Witty Butcher's Wife: Freud, Lacan, and the Conversion of Resistance to Theory." *Modern Language Notes* 102 (winter 1987): 989–1013.

Cixous, Hélène, and Catherine Clément. *The Newly Born Woman.* Trans. Betty Wing. Minneapolis: University of Minnesota Press, 1986.

Clark, Stuart. "Protestant Demonology: Sin, Superstition, and Society, 1520–1630." In *Early Modern European Witchcraft: Centres and Peripheries,* ed. Bengt Ankarloo and Gustav Henningsen. Oxford: Clarendon, 1993.

Clément, Catherine. "Sorceress and Hysteric." In Hélène Cixous and Catherine Clément, *The Newly Born Woman.* Trans. Betsy Wing. Minneapolis: University of Minnesota Press, 1986.

Clements, Robert. *Michelangelo's Theory of Art.* New York: New York University Press, 1961.

Copjec, Joan. "Vampires, Breast-Feeding, and Anxiety." *October* 58 (fall 1991): 25–43.

## Works Cited

Corrigan, Philip and Derek Sayer. *The Great Arch: English State Formation as Cultural Revolution*. Oxford: Blackwell, 1985.

Cotta, John. *The Triall of Witch-craft, shewing the True and Right Methode of Discovery*. 1616. Reprint, Amsterdam: Da Capo, 1968.

Craigie, James, ed. *Minor Works of King James VI and I*. Edinburgh: Scottish Text Society, 1988.

Crewe, Jonathan. *Trials of Authorship: Anterior Forms and Poetic Reconstruction from Wyatt to Shakespeare*. Berkeley: University of California Press, 1990.

Crooke, Helkiah. *Mikrocosmographia: A Description of the Body of Man*. London, 1618.

Hubert Damisch. *The Origin of Perspective*. Trans. John Goodman. Cambridge, MA: MIT Press, 1995.

———. "The Museum Device: Notes on Institutional Changes." *Lotus International* 35 (1982): 4–11.

Dante Alighieri, *The Inferno*. Trans. John Sinclair. New York: Oxford University Press, 1974.

Daston, Lorraine. "Baconian Facts and the Prehistory of Objectivity." In *Rethinking Objectivity*, ed. Allan Megill. Durham, NC: Duke University Press, 1994.

———. "The Factual Sensibility." *Isis* 79, no. 298 (1988): 452–67.

———. "Marvelous Facts and Miraculous Evidence in Early Modern Europe." *Critical Inquiry* 18 (1991): 93–124.

——— and Katherine Park. *Wonders and the Order of Nature: 1150–1750*. New York: Zone Books, 1998.

de Certeau, Michel. *The Writing of History*. Trans. Tom Conley. New York: Columbia University Press, 1988.

de Grazia, Margreta, Maureen Quilligan, and Peter Stallybrass, eds. *Subject and Object in Renaissance Culture*. Cambridge: Cambridge University Press, 1996.

de Grazia, Margreta and Peter Stallybrass. "The Materiality of the Shakespearean Text," *Shakespeare Quarterly* 44 (1993): 255–83.

de Man, Paul. *The Resistance to Theory*. Minneapolis: University of Minnesota Press, 1986.

Demos, John. *Entertaining Satan: Witchcraft and the Culture of Early New England*. Oxford: Oxford University Press, 1982.

Derrida, Jacques. "*Fors:* The Anglish Words of Nicolas Abraham and Maria Torok." Trans. Barbara Johnson. In Nicolas Abraham and Maria Torok, *The Wolf Man's Magic Word: A Cryptonymy*. Trans. Nicholas Rand. Minneapolis: University of Minnesota Press, 1986.

de Tolnay, Charles. *Michelangelo*. Vol. 5. Princeton: Princeton University Press, 1960.

Didi-Huberman, Georges. *Fra Angelico: Dissemblance and Figuration.* Trans. Jane Marie Todd. Chicago: University of Chicago Press, 1995.

*The disclosing of a late counterfeyted possession by the devyl in two maydens within the Citie of London.* 1574. Reprinted in *Witchcraft in England, 1558–1618.* Amherst: University of Massachusetts, 1991.

Dolar, Mladen. "'I Shall Be with You on Your Wedding Night': Lacan and the Uncanny." *October* 58 (fall 1991): 5–23.

Dollimore, Jonathan. *Radical Tragedy: Religion, Ideology, and Power in the Drama of Shakespeare and His Contemporaries.* 2d ed. Durham, NC: Duke University Press, 1993.

Eagleton, Terry. *William Shakespeare.* Oxford: Blackwell, 1986.

Edgerton, Samuel. *The Renaissance Discovery of Linear Perspective.* New York: Basic Books, 1975.

Eliot, T. S. *The Sacred Wood.* London: Methuen, 1960.

Erasmus, Desiderius. *Proverbes of Erasmus.* Trans. Richard Taverner. London, 1545.

Erlich, Avi. *Hamlet's Absent Father.* Princeton: Princeton University Press, 1977.

Evans, G. Blakemore, ed. *The Riverside Shakespeare.* Boston: Houghton Mifflin, 1974.

Felman, Shoshana, ed. *Literature and Psychoanalysis: The Question of Reading, Otherwise.* New Haven, CT: Yale French Studies, 1977.

Felperin, Howard. *Shakespearean Representation: Mimesis and Modernity in Elizabethan Tragedy.* Princeton, NJ: Princeton University Press, 1977.

Ferguson, Margaret. "Hamlet: Letters and Spirits." In *Shakespeare and the Question of Theory,* ed. Patricia Parker and Geoffrey Hartman. New York: Methuen, 1985.

Findlen, Paula. "Jokes of Nature and Jokes of Knowledge: The Playfulness of Scientific Discourse in Early Modern Europe." *Renaissance Quarterly* 43 (summer 1990): 292–331.

Flesch, William. *Generosity and the Limits of Authority: Shakespeare, Herbert, Milton.* Ithaca, NY: Cornell University Press, 1992.

———. "Proximity and Power: Shakespeare and Cinematic Space." *Theatre Journal* 39 (1987): 277–93.

Foster, Hal. "The Art of Fetishism: Notes on Dutch Still Life." In *Fetishism as Cultural Discourse,* ed. Emily Apter and William Pietz. Ithaca, NY: Cornell University Press, 1993.

———, ed. *Vision and Visuality.* Seattle: Bay, 1988.

Foucault, Michel. *The History of Sexuality, Volume I, An Introduction.* Trans. Robert Hurley. New York: Pantheon, 1978.

———. "Prose of the World." In *The Order of Things: An Archaeology of the Human Sciences.* New York: Vintage, 1973.

Works Cited

Freedman, Barbara. *Staging the Gaze: Postmodernism, Psychoanalysis, and Shakespearean Comedy.* Ithaca, NY: Cornell University Press, 1991.
Freud, Sigmund. "Fetishism." In *The Standard Edition of the Complete Psychological Works of Sigmund Freud,* ed. James Strachey. Vol. 21. London: Hogarth, 1961.
―――. "Mourning and Melancholia." In *The Standard Edition of the Complete Psychological Works of Sigmund Freud,* ed. James Strachey. Vol. 14. London: Hogarth, 1961.
Garber, Marjorie. *Shakespeare's Ghost Writers: Literature as Uncanny Causality.* New York: Methuen, 1987.
Garrett, Clarke. "Women and Witches: Patterns of Analysis." *Signs* 3 (1977): 461–70.
Gifford, George. *A Dialogue Concerning Witches and Witchcraftes.* 1593. Reprint, London: Oxford University Press.
Girard, René. "Hamlet's Dull Revenge." In *Literary Theory/Renaissance Texts,* ed. Patricia Parker and David Quint. Baltimore, MD: Johns Hopkins University Press, 1986.
―――. " 'To Entrap the Wisest': A Reading of *The Merchant of Venice.*" In *Literature and Society: Selected Papers from the English Institute,* ed. Edward Said. Baltimore, MD: Johns Hopkins University Press, 1980.
―――. *Violence and the Sacred.* Trans. Patrick Gregory. Baltimore, MD: Johns Hopkins University Press, 1972.
Godzich, Wlad. "In-Quest of Modernity." Foreword to Michael Nerlich. *Ideology of Adventure: Studies in Modern Consciousness, 1100–1750.* Vol. 1. Trans. Ruth Crowley. Minneapolis: University of Minnesota Press, 1987.
Goldberg, Jonathan. *Sodometries: Renaissance Texts, Modern Sexualities.* Stanford: Stanford University Press, 1992.
―――. "Perspectives: Dover Cliff and the Conditions of Representation." In *Shakespeare and Deconstruction,* G. Douglas Atkins and David Bergeron. New York: Peter Lang, 1988.
Gosson, Stephen. *The School of Abuse.* London: Shakespeare Society, 1841.
Granville-Barker, Harvey. *Prefaces to Shakespeare:* Hamlet. London: Sidgwick and Jackson, 1937.
Green, Andrew J. "The Cunning of the Scene." *Shakespeare Quarterly* 4, no. 4 (October 1953): 395–404.
Greenblatt, Stephen. "Meaning and Mutilation." In *The Body in Parts: Fantasies of Corporeality in Early Modern Europe,* ed. David Hillman and Carla Mazzio. New York: Routledge, 1997.
―――. *Shakespearean Negotiations: The Circulation of Social Energy in Renaissance England.* Berkeley: University of California Press, 1988.
―――. "Psychoanalysis and Renaissance Culture." In *Literary Theory/Re-*

*naissance Texts,* ed. Patricia Parker and David Quint. Baltimore: Johns Hopkins University Press, 1986.

———. *Renaissance Self-Fashioning: From More to Shakespeare.* Chicago: The University of Chicago Press, 1980.

Greg, W. W. "Hamlet's Hallucination." *Modern Language Review* 12, no. 4 (October 1917): 393–421.

Habermas, Jürgen. *The Structural Transformation of the Public Sphere.* Trans. Thomas Burger. Cambridge, MA: MIT Press, 1991.

Halpern, Richard. *The Poetics of Primitive Accumulation: English Renaissance Culture and the Genealogy of Capital.* Ithaca, NY: Cornell University Press, 1991.

Hanson, Elizabeth. *Discovering the Subject in Renaissance England.* Cambridge: Cambridge University Press, 1998.

Hawkes, Terence. "Telmah." In *Shakespeare and the Question of Theory,* ed. Patricia Parker and Geoffrey Hartman. New York: Methuen, 1985.

Heckscher, William. *Rembrandt's Anatomy of Dr. Nicolaas Tulp.* New York: New York University Press, 1958.

Hertz, Neil. *The End of the Line.* New York: Columbia University Press, 1985.

Hodges, Devon. *Renaissance Fictions of Anatomy.* Amherst: University of Massachusetts Press, 1985.

Howard, Jean. "The New Historicism in Renaissance Studies." *English Literary Renaissance* 16, no. 1 (1986): 13–43.

Imperato, Ferrante. *Dell'Historia Naturale di Ferante Imperato Napolitano Libri XXVII Nella quale ordinatamente si tratta della diversa condition di miniere, e pietre. Con alcune histoire di Piante, et Animali; sin' hora non date in luce.* Naples, 1599.

Irigaray, Luce. *This Sex Which Is Not One.* Trans. Catherine Porter. Ithaca, NY: Cornell University Press, 1985.

James I. *Daemonologie.* In *Minor Works of King James VI and I,* ed. James Craigie. Edinburgh: Scottish Text Society, 1982.

Jay, Martin. "Scopic Regimes of Modernity." In *Vision and Visuality,* ed. Hal Foster. Seattle: Bay, 1988.

Jones, Ernest. *Hamlet and Oedipus.* New York: Norton, 1949.

———. "The Death of Hamlet's Father." *International Journal of Psychoanalysis* 29 (1948): 174–77.

Kahn, Coppélia. "The Absent Mother in *King Lear.*" In *Rewriting the Renaissance: The Discourse of Sexual Difference in Early Modern Europe,* ed. Margaret Ferguson, Maureen Quilligan, and Nancy Vickers. Chicago: University of Chicago Press, 1986.

Kamps, Ivo, ed. *Materialist Shakespeare: A History.* London: Verso, 1995.

Kantorowicz, Ernst. *The King's Two Bodies: A Study in Medieval Political Theology.* Princeton: Princeton University Press, 1957.

Kastan, David Scott. "'His semblable is his mirror': Hamlet and the Imitation of Revenge." *Shakespeare Studies* 19 (1987): 111–24.

Keenan, Thomas. "The Point is to (Ex)Change It." In *Fetishism as Cultural Discourse*, ed. Emily Apter and William Pietz. Ithaca, NY: Cornell University Press, 1993.

Kenseth, Joy. "'A World of Wonders in One Closet Shut.'" In *The Age of the Marvelous*, ed. Joy Kenseth. Hanover, NH: Hood Museum of Art–Dartmouth College, 1991.

Knapp, Jeffrey. *An Empire Nowhere: England, America, and Literature from Utopia to* The Tempest. Berkeley: University of California Press, 1992.

Kristeva, Julia. "Freud and Love: Treatment and Its Discontents." In *The Kristeva Reader*, ed. Toril Moi. New York: Columbia University Press, 1986.

———. *Powers of Horror: An Essay on Abjection*. New York: Columbia University Press, 1982.

Lacan, Jacques. "Desire and the Interpretation of Desire in *Hamlet*." In *Literature and Psychoanalysis: The Question of Reading, Otherwise*, ed. Shoshana Felman. New Haven, CT: Yale French Studies, 1977.

———. *Ecrits: A Selection*. Trans. Alan Sheridan. New York: Norton, 1977.

———. *Four Fundamental Concepts of Psychoanalysis*. Trans. Alan Sheridan. New York: Norton, 1977.

———. *The Seminar of Jacques Lacan: Book VII: The Ethics of Psychoanalysis, 1959–1960*. Ed. J.-A. Miller. Trans. Dennis Porter. New York: Norton, 1992.

Laclau, Ernesto. *New Reflections on the Revolution of Our Time*. London: Verso, 1990.

——— and Chantal Mouffe. *Hegemony and Socialist Strategy: Towards a Radical Democratic Politics*. London: Verso, 1985.

Laplanche, Jean and J.-B. Pontalis. "Fantasy and the Origins of Sexuality." In *Formations of Fantasy*, ed. Victor Burgin, James Donald, and Cora Kaplan (London: Methuen, 1986), 5–27.

——— and J.-B. Pontalis, eds. *The Language of Psychoanalysis*. Trans. D. Nicholson-Smith. New York: Norton, 1973.

Laqueur, Thomas. *Making Sex: Body and Gender from the Greeks to Freud*. Cambridge, MA: Harvard University Press, 1990.

Larner, Christina. *Witchcraft and Religion: The Politics of Popular Belief*. Oxford: Basil Blackwell, 1984.

Leech, Clifford. "The Hesitation of Pyrrhus." In *The Morality of Art: Essays Presented to G. Wilson Knight*, ed. D. W. Jefferson. New York: Barnes and Noble, 1969.

Lefort, Claude. *The Political Forms of Modern Society: Bureaucracy, Democracy, Totalitarianism*. Ed. John Thompson. Cambridge, MA: MIT Press, 1986.

Levack, Brian. *The Witch-Hunt in Early Modern Europe*. London: Longman, 1987.

Levin, Harry. *The Question of* Hamlet. New York: Viking, 1959.

Levine, Laura. "Men in Women's Clothing: Anti-theatricality and Effeminization from 1579 to 1642." *Criticism* 28 (1986): 121–43.

Lobanov-Rostovsky, Sergei. "Taming the Basilisk." In *The Body in Parts: Fantasies of Corporeality in Early Modern Europe,* ed. David Hillman and Carla Mazzio. New York: Routledge, 1997.

Lugli, Adalgisa. *Naturalia et Mirabilia. Il collezionismo enciclopedico nelle Wunderkammern d'Europa.* Milan: Mazzotta, 1990.

Lukacher, Ned. "Anamorphic Stuff: Shakespeare, Catharsis, Lacan." *The South Atlantic Quarterly* 88 (fall 1989): 870–75.

———. *Primal Scenes: Literature, Philosophy, Psychoanalysis.* Ithaca, NY: Cornell University Press, 1986.

Lupton, Julia Reinhard. *Afterlives of the Saints: Hagiography, Typology, and Renaissance Literature.* Stanford: Stanford University Press, 1996.

Lupton, Julia, and Kenneth Reinhard. *After Oedipus: Shakespeare in Psychoanalysis.* Ithaca, NY: Cornell University Press, 1993.

———. "Shapes of Grief: Freud, *Hamlet,* and Mourning," *Genders* 4 (March 1989): 50–67.

Macfarlane, Thomas. *Witchcraft in Tudor and Stuart England: A Regional and Comparative Study.* London: Routledge and Kegan Paul, 1970.

Marchitello, Howard. "Vesalius' *Fabrica* and Shakespeare's *Othello:* Anatomy, Gender, and the Narrative Production of Meaning." *Criticism* 35, no. 4 (fall 1993): 529–58.

Marcus, Leah. *Puzzling Shakespeare.* Berkeley: University of California Press, 1988.

Marx, Karl. *Capital: A Critique of Political Economy.* Vol. 1. Trans. Ben Fowkes. New York: Vintage, 1977.

———. *Collected Works.* Vol. 3. London: Lawrence and Wishart, 1976.

Masten, Jeffrey. *Textual Intercourse: Collaboration, Authorship, and Sexualities in Renaissance Drama.* Cambridge: Cambridge University Press, 1997.

Maus, Katharine Eisaman. *Inwardness and Theater in the English Renaissance.* Chicago: University of Chicago Press, 1995.

Mercati, Michele. *Metallotheca: Opus Posthumum.* Rome, 1717.

McMillin, Scott. "Shakespeare's Troy: The Space of Narcissism and Theatre." Typescript, Cornell University: 1987.

———. "Can Hamlet be Cured?" Typescript, Cornell University: 1987.

Megill, Allan, ed. *Rethinking Objectivity.* Durham, NC: Duke University Press, 1994.

Miller, David. *The Novel and the Police.* Berkeley: University of California Press, 1988.

Misselden, Edward. *The Circle of Commerce.* 1623. Reprint, New York: Augustus Kelley, 1971.

Muchembled, Robert. "Satanic Myths and Cultural Reality." In *Early Modern European Witchcraft: Centres and Peripheries,* ed. Bengt Ankarloo and Gustav Henningsen. Oxford: Clarendon, 1993.

Mullaney, Steven. *The Place of the Stage: License, Play, and Power in Renaissance England.* Chicago: University of Chicago Press, 1988.

Munday, Anthony. *A Second and Third Blast of Retrait from Plaies and Theaters.* 1580. Reprint, New York: Garland, 1973.

Murray, Timothy. "Translating Montaigne's Crypts: Melancholic Relations and the Sites of Altarbiography." In *Repossessions: Psychoanalysis and the Phantasms of Early Modern Culture,* ed. Murray and Smith. Minneapolis: University of Minnesota Press, 1998.

—————— and Alan K. Smith, eds. *Repossessions: Psychoanalysis and the Phantasms of Early Modern Culture.* Minneapolis: University of Minnesota Press, 1998.

Nashe, Thomas. *Pierce Penniless's Supplication to the Devil.* 1592. Reprint, London: Shakespeare Society, 1842.

Neill, Michael. *Issues of Death: Mortality and Identity in English Renaissance Tragedy.* Oxford: Oxford University Press, 1997.

Newman, Karen. *Fashioning Femininity and English Renaissance Drama.* Chicago: University of Chicago Press, 1991.

——————. "City Talk: Women and Commodification in Jonson's *Epicoene.*" *English Literary History* 56 (summer 1989): 503–18.

Olmi, Giuseppe. "Science–Honour–Metaphor: Italian Cabinets of the Sixteenth and Seventeenth Centuries." In *The Origins of Museums: The Cabinets of Curiosities in Sixteenth and Seventeenth-Century Europe,* ed. Oliver Impey and Arthur MacGregor. Oxford: Clarendon, 1985.

O'Malley, C. D. *Andreas Vesalius of Brussels, 1514–1564.* Berkeley: University of California, 1965.

Orgel, Stephen. "Nobody's Perfect: Or, Why Did the English Stage Take Boys for Women?" In *Displacing Homophobia,* ed. Ronald Butters, John Clum, and Michael Moon. (Durham, NC: Duke University Press, 1989).

——————. *The Illusion of Power.* Berkeley: University of California Press, 1975.

Osborne, Harold. *The Oxford Companion to Art.* London: Oxford University Press, 1970.

Panofsky, Erwin. *Early Netherlandish Painting: Its Origins and Character.* Vol. 1. Cambridge, MA: Harvard University Press, 1953.

Parker, Patricia. *Shakespeare from the Margins: Language, Culture, Context.* Chicago: University of Chicago Press, 1996.

—————— and Geoffrey Hartman, eds. *Shakespeare and the Question of Theory.* New York: Methuen, 1985.

Pietz, William. "The Problem of the Fetish, I." *Res* 9 (spring 1985): 5–17.

Pomian, Krzysztof. *Collectors and Curiosities: Paris and Venice, 1500–1800.* Trans. Elizabeth Wiles-Portier. Cambridge: Polity, 1990.

Pye, Christopher. *The Regal Phantasm: Shakespeare and the Politics of Spectacle.* London: Routledge, 1990.

Rank, Otto. "The Play within the Play in *Hamlet.*" Trans. Paul Lewison. *Journal of the Otto Rank Association* 6, no. 2 (December 1971): 5–21.

Rankins, William. *A Mirror of Monsters.* London, 1587.

Robson, W. W. "Did the King See the Dumb-Show?" *Cambridge Quarterly* 6 (1972–75): 303–25.

Roper, Lyndal. "Exorcism and the Theology of the Body." In *Oedipus and the Devil: Witchcraft, Sexuality, and Religion in Early Modern Europe.* London: Routledge, 1994.

Rorty, Richard. *Philosophy and the Mirror of Nature.* Princeton, NJ: Princeton University Press, 1979.

Rose, Jacqueline. *States of Fantasy.* Oxford: Clarendon, 1996.

Rosen, Barbara, ed. *Witchcraft in England, 1558–1618.* Amherst: University of Massachusetts Press, 1991.

Rotman, Brian. *Signifying Nothing: The Semiotics of Nothing.* New York: St. Martin's, 1987.

Sawday, Jonathan. *The Body Emblazoned: Dissection and the Human Body in Renaissance Culture.* London: Routledge, 1995.

Schlegel, A. W. *A Course of Lectures on Dramatic Art and Literature.* Trans. John Black. London: Bell and Daldy, 1871.

Schupbach, William. "Collections of Curiosities in Academic Institutions." In *The Origins of Museums: The Cabinets of Curiosities in Sixteenth and Seventeenth-Century Europe,* ed. Oliver Impey and Arthur MacGregor. Oxford: Clarendon Press, 1985.

Scot, Reginald. *The Discoverie of Witchcraft.* 1584. Reprint, New York: Dover, 1972.

Sedgwick, Eve Kosofsky. *Between Men: English Literature and Male Homo-social Desire.* New York: Columbia University Press, 1985.

Shakespeare, William. *Antony and Cleopatra.* Ed. Frank Kermode. In *The Riverside Shakespeare,* ed. G. Blakemore Evans, et al. Boston: Houghton Mifflin, 1974.

———. *Hamlet.* Ed. Frank Kermode. In *The Riverside Shakespeare,* ed. G. Blakemore Evans, et al. Boston: Houghton Mifflin, 1974.

———. *Hamlet.* Ed. Horace Furness. 4 vols. In *A New Variorum Edition of Shakespeare,* ed. Horace H. Furness. 29 vols. Philadelphia: Lippincott, 1877.

———. *Henry VI, Part 1.* Ed. Herschel Baker. *The Riverside Shakespeare,* ed. G. Blakemore Evans, et al. Boston: Houghton Mifflin, 1974.

———. *Julius Caesar.* Ed. Frank Kermode. *The Riverside Shakespeare,* ed. G. Blakemore Evans, et al. Boston: Houghton Mifflin, 1974.

————. *King Lear.* Ed. Kenneth Muir. *The Arden Shakespeare.* London: Routledge, 1991.

————. *The Rape of Lucrece.* Ed. Hallett Smith. *The Riverside Shakespeare,* ed. G. Blakemore Evans, et al. Boston: Houghton Mifflin, 1974.

————. *The Tempest.* Ed. Hallett Smith. *Riverside Shakespeare,* ed. G. Blakemore Evans et al. Boston: Houghton Mifflin, 1974.

Shelton, Anthony Alan. "Cabinets of Transgression: Renaissance Collections and the Incorporation of the New World." In *The Cultures of Collecting,* ed. John Elsner and Roger Cardinal. London: Reaktion, 1994.

Skinner, Quentin. *The Foundations of Modern Political Thought.* Vol. 2. Cambridge: Cambridge University Press, 1978.

Snyder, Susan. *The Comic Matrix of Shakespeare's Tragedies.* Princeton, NJ: Princeton University Press, 1979.

Stafford, Barbara Maria. *Artful Science: Enlightenment, Entertainment, and the Eclipse of Visual Education.* Cambridge, MA: MIT Press, 1994.

Stallybrass, Peter. "Macbeth and Witchcraft." In *Focus on* Macbeth, ed. J. R. Brown. London: Routledge and Kegan Paul, 1982.

Steinberg, Leo. "A Corner of *The Last Judgment.*" *Daedalus* 109 (spring 1980): 207–73.

————. "The Line of Fate in Michelangelo's Painting." *Critical Inquiry* 6 (Spring 1980): 411–54.

Stow, John. *Annales of England.* 1600. Reprinted in *Witchcraft in England, 1558–1618,* ed. Barbara Rosen. Amherst: University of Massachusetts Press, 1991.

Stubbes, Philip. *The Anatomie of Abuses,* ed. Arthur Freeman. 1583. Reprint, London: Garland Press, 1973.

Taylor, Charles. *Sources of the Self: The Making of Modern Identity.* Cambridge, MA: Harvard University Press, 1989.

Thomas, Keith. *Religion and the Decline of Magic.* New York: Scribners, 1971.

*A true and particular observation of a notable piece of witchcraft practised by John Samuel, . . . Alice Samuel, . . . and Agnes Samuel . . . of Warboys.* 1589. Reprinted in *Witchcraft in England, 1558–1618,* ed. Barbara Rosen. Amherst: University of Massachusetts Press, 1991.

Valverdi, Juan de. *Anatomia del Corporo Humano.* Rome: n.p., 1560.

Veeser, H. Aram. "Introduction." In *The New Historicism,* ed. H. Aram Veeser. New York: Routledge, 1989.

Vesalius, Andreas. *De Humani Corporis.* Amsterdam, 1642.

Virgil. *The Aeneid.* In *Virgili Maronis Opera,* ed. F. A. Hirtzel. Oxford: Oxford University Press, 1966.

Wayne, Don. "Drama and Society in the Age of Jonson: An Alternative View." *Renaissance Drama* 13 (summer 1982): 103–29.

## Works Cited

Wayne, Valerie, ed. *The Matter of Difference: Materialist Feminist Criticism of Shakespeare*. Ithaca, NY: Cornell University Press, 1991.

Weber, Max. "The Sociology of Charismatic Authority." In *From Max Weber: Essays in Sociology*, ed. H. H. Gerth and C. Wright Mills. New York: Oxford University Press, 1946.

Weyer. Johann. *De praestigiis daemonum*. In *Witches, Devils, and Doctors in the Renaissance: Johann Weyer,* De praestigiis daemonum, ed. George Mora. Trans. John Shea. Binghamton, NY: Medieval and Renaissance Texts and Studies, 1991.

White, John. *The Birth and Rebirth of Pictorial Space.* 3d edition. Cambridge, MA: Belknap, 1987.

Wilson, J. Dover. *What Happens in* Hamlet. Cambridge: Cambridge University Press, 1964.

Yates, Frances. *The Art of Memory.* Harmondsworth, England: Penguin, 1969.

Žižek, Slavoj. "Grimaces of the Real, or When the Phallus Appears." *October* 58 (fall 1991): 45–68.

———. *Looking Awry: An Introduction to Jacques Lacan through Popular Culture.* Cambridge, MA: MIT Press, 1991.

———. *The Sublime Object of Ideology.* London: Verso, 1989.

# Index

*Locators in italics indicate illustrations.*

Christopher Pye is Professor and Chair in the Department of English at Williams College. He is the author of *The Regal Phantasm: Shakespeare and the Politics of Spectacle.*

Library of Congress Cataloging-in-Publication Data

Pye, Christopher

The vanishing : Shakespeare, the subject, and early modern culture / Christopher Pye.

p.   cm.

Includes bibliographical references and index.

ISBN 0-8223-2510-1 (alk. paper) — ISBN 0-8223-2547-0 (pbk. : alk. paper)

1. Shakespeare, William, 1564–1616 — Tragedies.

2. Shakespeare, William, 1564–1616. Hamlet.

3. Shakespeare, William, 1564–1616. King Lear.

4. Michelangelo Buonarroti, 1475–1564. Last Judgment.

5. Psychoanalysis and culture.   6. Subjectivity in literature.

7. Civilization, Modern.   8. Subjectivity in art.   9. Self in literature.   10. Renaissance.   I. Title.

PR2983 .P94   2000

822.3'3

99-050752